ACKNOWLEDGMENTS

So many people have supported my interest and education in dog behavior along the way that it would be impossible to list them all here. I do want to give special thanks to our local pet obedience instructor Marta Spry, who was unfailingly patient and helpful when I was a dog-crazy child with big dreams and a thousand questions.

I also want to thank a few amazing educators at the Ohio State University College of Veterinary Medicine, whose tremendous wealth of knowledge was a great resource during my years as a student there: Traci Shreyer, a wonderful applied animal behaviorist who is as kind to students and pet owners as she is to the dogs she works with; Debby Miller, the puppy kindergarten instructor who patiently allowed me to become a permanent fixture in her classes for four straight years; and Dr. Meghan Herron, OSU's board-certified veterinary behaviorist who was always up for questions and discussion about any of her current cases.

Thank you as well to each and every one of my behavioral clients and patients over the years. I have learned something from every dog that has ever crossed my path, and I owe all of them—and their owners—a great debt of gratitude.

CONTENTS

PART III
COOPERATIVE K9s
TRAINING FOR HANDLING AND BASIC CARE **115**

PART IV
JUST FOR FUN
TRICKS AND GAMES **137**

PART V
TROUBLE IN PARADISE
UNDERSTANDING AND ADDRESSING BEHAVIORAL PROBLEMS 165

INTRODUCTION

If you've picked up this book and decided to glance through the pages, chances are you have some questions about how to train your dog. Welcome to the club—you're in good company!

The truth is, virtually every dog owner will run into a behavioral concern or a training problem at some point in their pup's life. This is entirely normal. Dogs are amazing creatures, but they don't come preprogrammed with an understanding of human rules and expectations—and they don't speak English, so teaching them what we want can be a challenge.

Figuring out how to wrangle your wild-eyed, barking, leash-pulling furry friend into a polite and well-mannered companion can seem like a daunting task at first. Fortunately, the solutions are often simpler than you might think; you just need a clear training plan and a little motivation.

My goal in the pages that follow is to provide you with simple, actionable training solutions for a variety of common problems. Really—that's it! No long, technical dissertations on the intricate minutiae of learning theory or complicated twelve-week programs designed to transform your life and that of your pet. These things have their place, but I want this book to be something different.

And this "something different" is easy to read and addresses your needs without wasting your time.

As you will see, each of the following sections is devoted to an area of concern that might interest you, ranging from a quick crash course on dog training in general to specific advice on common training issues and basic obedience, handling and grooming, tricks and games, and even higher-level behavioral concerns such as aggression and anxiety.

I should stress that although a lot of the training described here is for older dogs, there's plenty of training for younger dogs too. After all, puppies are just starting out in life, and they've got plenty to learn! Maybe you are the proud owners of a new puppy and want to know how to get your little boy or girl ready for life. Or maybe you have an older dog who may have developed some bad habits you would like to change. In every case, you will find a targeted, practical step-by-step training plan to tackle the issue or problem. So whether you're concerned about nuisance behaviors like begging at the table or chewing on furniture, more serious issues like getting into fights or biting visitors, or just want to teach your dog some easy obedience skills, this book is for you.

Whatever your specific problem might be, I hope you'll find this resource helpful!

Best wishes,
Jennifer L. Summerfield, DVM, CPDT-KA

PART I
THE BASICS
WHAT EVERY DOG OWNER NEEDS TO KNOW

First, a few words on all of this training stuff—how to motivate your dog, general suggestions on techniques and equipment, and a tiny bit of behavioral science.

But wait, you might say! This all sounds suspiciously dull and irrelevant to my situation...I just want to know how to fix my dog's problem with X, Y, or Z.

Believe me, I understand—don't worry! We'll get there. As promised, the biggest chunk of this book will be devoted to giving you practical solutions for whatever behavioral issue or concern you're currently facing with your dog.

But if we want to be able to solve your training problems effectively, a little background knowledge is important. Don't skip over it, as tempting as it might be! You don't need a degree in behavioral science to successfully teach your dog to stop jumping on guests, but there are a few basic things you should know.

Namely, how does your dog actually learn things? What works well and what doesn't when it comes to rewards and corrections? And what "tricks of the trade" can you use to make life easier while you're working on the problem?

We'll stick to the info that's interesting and useful for everyday life and save the scientific literature reviews and philosophical musings for another time... So hang in there and read on.

It'll be a good use of your time, I promise.

HOW DOGS LEARN

There is a single, vital, and inarguable tenet of dog behavior (and, indeed, all animal behavior!) that every effective trainer knows. It's central to designing a good training plan, but it might require you to let go of some preconceived notions about your pup and his views of the world.

Are you ready?

Here it is:

Dogs do what works.

Period. End of story.

If you understand this basic truth, you're at least 75 percent of the way toward solving your training issues—so take a moment to really wrap your head around what this means.

It means, essentially, that behavior that is rewarded will be repeated. And behavior that doesn't pay off will tend to die out. Dogs are highly adaptable creatures; they are quick to learn what works and what doesn't and will adjust their future behavior accordingly.

An example:

Let's say that Buddy puts his paws up on the kitchen counter, finds a steak defrosting there, and eats the entire thing. A great day for Buddy, although his owner is likely not pleased. From his perspective, Buddy's learned that putting his paws on the counter was incredibly rewarding, so it's likely that he'll try this behavior again in the future.

On the other hand, if Buddy's owner is diligent about making sure that food is put away, the dog may not find anything at all if he puts his paws up on the counter. If this happens a few times, he'll eventually stop trying. He's learned that jumping up on the counter doesn't lead to anything particularly fun or interesting. So why bother doing it?

Note that in this example, punishment plays no role at all in stopping the unwanted behavior. This is surprising for many dog owners. Punishing Buddy after the fact, in this case, would do no good at all—he's already been "rewarded" (by eating the steak) for his counter surfing behavior, so a scolding or swat on the nose will do nothing to dissuade him next time.

This is dog training, in a nutshell.

Your job as a trainer is to make sure that "good" behavior is handsomely rewarded in some way or another, and that "bad" or unwanted behavior (from our perspective) doesn't lead to anything your dog likes. This is sometimes easier said than done, of course! But it should always be your goal.

Your dog, for his part, has no understanding of good or bad behavior in a moral sense. So when he does something you don't like, from jumping up on your guests to pooping in the house, remember that he isn't being "naughty." He just doesn't know what you want, or you haven't made it worth his while to care.

Take a deep breath, and let's figure out how you can teach him.

USING REWARDS EFFECTIVELY

Now you know that you need to reward your dog for doing things you like. Pretty simple, right?

So let's talk about rewards.

For our purposes in this book, we'll focus primarily on food rewards. This means that you'll give your dog a treat of some kind when he does what you ask. This treat could be anything from dry kibble or Milk-Bones, to soft smelly store-bought treats, or even human food like chicken or roast beef.

Why use food, you might ask?

This is a very reasonable question, and one that my beginner students ask frequently in our obedience classes. There are several factors that make food treats a great choice for training:

- They're convenient and user-friendly. It's very easy to carry a baggie full of tasty snacks in your pocket so that food is always available if you need it.
- Treats can be used in a very precise way. You want to provide a reward the exact moment your dog does what you're asking. This is much harder to do with other types of rewards, and good timing is critically important for learning.
- They help to build a positive association for whatever you're teaching, since most dogs love to eat. If you want your pup to enjoy working with you, giving him a piece of cheese every time he listens will go a long way toward convincing him that this "training" thing is lots of fun.
- Last but not least...*they work*. Used properly, food rewards are arguably the most effective tool at your disposal for teaching new behaviors—so take advantage of them, especially in the early stages of training.

What about other types of rewards? Do we have any other options besides food?

Yes, most definitely! Anything that your dog enjoys can be a training reward, at least in theory—the tricky part is figuring out how to make this work.

Toys and various types of play (including tug-of-war, fetch, and chase games) are often used as rewards in dog sports such as agility and competitive obedience, especially when the handler wants more speed and enthusiasm for a particular behavior. *But*—and this is a big "but"—it takes quite a bit more skill and experience to use these rewards effectively, and they're much less practical for teaching new behaviors to a novice dog.

So if you're fairly new to training, I strongly suggest you stick with treats for now. Later on, you can branch out a bit, especially if you decide to get involved in competitive dog sports, search and rescue work, and other activities that may require more energy and drive.

Following are a few general tips for using food rewards effectively:

- *Vary the types of treats you're using, depending on the task.* For really challenging things, such as calling your dog away from a squirrel across an open field, use the big guns: hot dog slices or pieces of roast beef. If you're working on the "sit" command in your kitchen, it's fine to use leftover kibble from his dinner the night before.
- *Use small-sized treats or food cut into tiny pieces.* For most dogs, each treat should be no larger than a pea. This allows you to give lots of rewards in a single training session, without your dog filling up or getting fat.
- *Dogs are very literal—so what you reward is what you get.* Timing matters: if you're teaching a "sit" command, make sure to pop the treat into his mouth as soon as his rear end touches the floor. Too early or too late, and you'll accidentally reward standing up instead... which just muddies the water and confuses your dog.

WHAT ABOUT CORRECTIONS— USEFUL OR NOT?

In years past, it was thought that punishment for "bad" behavior was a necessary part of training dogs. Trainers often used choke collars, prong collars, and even electronic shock collars to correct unwanted behavior or to punish dogs for failing to obey a command.

Fortunately, as our understanding of behavioral science and animal learning has increased over the past few decades, we now know that harsh correction-based techniques like these are not needed for effective training. This is great news for dogs, and also for us as trainers!

I'm very happy to say that in the United States, every professional organization for educated trainers and behaviorists now recommends against the use of punishment in dog training, including the American Veterinary Society of Animal Behavior (AVSAB), the American College of Veterinary Behaviorists (ACVB), the Association of Professional Dog Trainers (APDT), and the Pet Professional Guild (PPG).

At first blush, this might seem puzzling. What's wrong with using corrections? Doesn't punishment for misbehavior help your dog learn faster?

You would think so, I know, but the truth is much more complicated.

It's not that punishment doesn't work, at least in some cases. It can certainly be successful at changing certain types of behavior. But there's a downside. Even when it's used effectively, punishment carries the risk of causing some unpleasant behavioral side effects:

- Your dog may associate the correction with something innocuous in the environment (or even with you, the owner), rather than with his behavior. This can result in your pup becoming afraid of you or of the backyard, visitors, his leash, or a variety of other things that he will now associate with pain or discomfort.
- Punishment increases stress and makes it more difficult for your dog to learn. This means that teaching a new behavior often takes much longer when corrections are used; it's hard to think when you're frightened or nervous.
- Using corrections to teach obedience skills can create a negative association with the training process, so that your dog is reluctant to engage with you. We all enjoy learning much more when it's a fun game with lots of rewards, rather than when it's a potential minefield of errors with scolding (or worse) when we make a mistake! Your pup is no different; if he's stressed and not having fun, training becomes a chore for both of you.
- With behavioral issues such as aggression, punishment often suppresses warning signs such as growling or snarling without actually

addressing the underlying issue, which is the dog's discomfort with the situation. This can result in the stereotypical "attack out of the blue," when your dog is pushed past his limit. It is a major reason that correction-based training methods are never recommended for aggressive dogs.

To avoid these issues, you're much better off focusing on what your dog is doing right. Show him what you want and reward him for doing what you ask. If he makes a mistake, just back up and try again, or change something in the environment to help him be successful.

CHOOSING YOUR GEAR: LEASHES, COLLARS, AND HARNESSES

If you've ever walked into a pet store or browsed online for training equipment, you are no doubt aware that there are lots of options available. The sheer array of choices can be overwhelming for many new dog owners, but don't worry—the list of things you need (or might need, depending on your dog) is actually fairly short.

For starters, your dog will need a **flat buckle collar**.

Plain or fancy, made of no-frills nylon or hand-embroidered leather, purchased at Walmart or from an online vendor on *Etsy*—the choice is entirely up to you! What matters is that it fits well and stays on. This is what you will attach your dog's ID tags to for everyday wear, and it can also be used for walks and training sessions.

Some dogs, particularly sighthounds and other breeds with small heads, may be able to back out of a buckle collar—even if it's well-fitted. If you're concerned about this possibility, try a **martingale collar** instead. These collars (also called limited slip collars) are made to tighten slightly if any tension is applied, which makes them much harder to slip out of.

If your dog has a sensitive neck or trachea, you could also consider a **body harness** for daily walks and training. These have the advantage of being comfortable for the dog, and most designs are also quite difficult to get out of—which is great for safety.

Harnesses are used most commonly for small dogs, since this type of harness has a tendency to encourage leash-pulling. This is not a major problem with a toy poodle, but it is less than ideal if you have an 80-pound Labrador retriever. This doesn't necessarily mean that you can't use a harness with a larger dog, of course, but you should be aware that it may make your loose-leash walk training a bit more challenging.

Now, what about leashes? Here, again, the options seem endless.

The truth is, there doesn't need to be anything complicated or difficult about choosing a training leash for your dog. In most cases, a **4- to 6-foot nylon or leather leash** is all you need.

There are certainly many other choices available, but for beginner dog training, whether in a class or at home, those choices will just make your life harder. Trust me on this. If you use anything shorter, your dog won't have room to move. With a longer leash, both of you will get tangled up. Chain leashes are hard on your hands and annoyingly heavy for your pup. Retractable leashes may have their place—mainly for relaxed leash walks in quiet, sparsely populated areas—but they're a logistical nightmare for training.

For transitioning to off-leash skills, practicing recalls, or giving your dog more freedom in wide open spaces, you may also want to invest in a long line. This is a very long (up to 50 feet or more) lightweight training leash that gives you some control over your dog at a distance. We will discuss some potential uses for a long line later in the book. For now, just keep it in your toolbox.

Do yourself a favor and stick with the basics. You can always look into fancier equipment later if you decide to get involved in more specialized types of training. For now, a simple leash and collar is all you need.

MANAGEMENT AND WHY IT MATTERS

This topic isn't as flashy or exciting as some of the others we're going to discuss, but bear with me for a few minutes, because it's incredibly important. In fact, I would go so far as to say that good management is the single most critical part of a successful training plan.

Management means proactively changing things in the environment to ensure that your dog isn't accidentally "practicing" bad behavior or being rewarded for things you don't want.

For example, if you want to train your dog not to jump on people, you might work on this problem each week in your obedience class. Which is great! Taking time to teach the behavior you want is important. *But*...what you do at home matters just as much, if not more. If your pup is continuing to jump all over every visitor who comes into the house, you'll never make any progress at all. No matter how many classes you take, or how good your obedience instructor is, it's all for naught.

Now, I realize that every time the doorbell rings you don't have time to leash your dog, grab your treats, remember what your instructor said, and launch into an impromptu training session. Fair enough. So what to do?

This is where management comes in.

Management, in this context, means that before answering the door you put your dog in another room with the door closed or behind a baby gate. This way, you can concentrate on your guests and your dog doesn't get to practice his jumping behavior. A win-win for both of you.

Another example: let's say you're teaching your dog to come when you call him. This is a very important skill, and one that's worth training well. In the early stages, when he's first learning, he may be reliable to come in the house or in your fenced backyard but still very distracted in other places.

In this case, management means keeping him on-leash at the park if you aren't sure he'll come when you call. This is important for safety reasons, but also to prevent your dog from "practicing" the behavior of ignoring you. If he sees a squirrel and takes off after it, and you call him, is he likely to stop and come back? If not, he shouldn't be off-leash—he's not ready yet.

Finally, it's important to note that management can be a perfectly reasonable long-term solution for some behavioral issues. If you have two dogs who fight over food, for example, it's probably simpler to just feed them in separate rooms as opposed to putting together a complicated training plan to try and teach them to eat side by side.

In dog training, as with so many things in life, you have to pick your battles. There's nothing wrong with avoiding the problem, if it can be easily managed this way.

EXERCISE AND MENTAL STIMULATION

These two areas, exercise and mental stimulation, are two of the most basic aspects of dog ownership and are often two of the most overlooked, in my experience. I know, life is busy. We all have a seemingly endless list of tasks and responsibilities to deal with each day, so it can be hard to find time for anything extra...whether it's a walk around the neighborhood, a trip to the park, or a weekend hike in the woods.

Unfortunately, though, these are things that really matter. If you're not providing your dog with adequate amounts of exercise (for both the body and the mind), you'll likely find your dog to be extremely hard to live with. When behavioral issues pop up, training can certainly help, but it's not a substitute for addressing your dog's basic needs.

At the risk of stating the obvious, dogs are dogs! That is to say, they are smart, energetic carnivores that have been bred for generations to do a variety of very active jobs. While there are still true working dogs out there who spend their days herding sheep, sniffing for contraband, or trailing game in the forest, the majority of our canine companions nowadays are pampered pets.

Our dogs typically spend more time snoozing on the sofa or getting lazy belly rubs than running, jumping, sniffing, or using their brains, which is fine, to a point. But even the most dedicated couch potato still needs an occasional opportunity to get out and be a dog. And if you have a particularly active breed, or a high-energy puppy who's easily bored, daily exercise is really nonnegotiable.

As the saying goes, a tired dog is a happy dog. Tired dogs are also much more well-behaved, on the whole; your pup will be far less inclined to bark excessively, dig in the yard, chew your furniture, or chase the kids if he's already pleasantly exhausted from other activities.

Fortunately, there are lots of things you can do to provide your dog a good workout—whether it's mental, physical, or both. Find some options that work for you, and make time each day to give your pup some exercise.

A few suggestions to help get you started:

GO FOR A WALK

Ah, the daily walk...a tried and true part of most dogs' daily exercise routine. This is a great starting point, as it's fairly easy to find twenty to thirty minutes each morning or evening to squeeze in a few laps around the block.

If you find that plodding along the same old stretch of sidewalk together doesn't tire your dog out as much as you would like, try taking him someplace less crowded and letting him roam around, sniff, and explore on a long line. Using a very long (up to 50 feet), lightweight training leash can give your pup some extra freedom. You might be surprised how much more he enjoys this and how much more tired he is when you get home.

DO SOME TRAINING

Remember, exercise doesn't have to mean physical activity. Many owners are surprised by how exhausted their dogs are after a training class or even after spending a few minutes at home working on a new skill. This is because learning takes a lot of energy. Consider signing up for a weekly obedience or agility class, or take up some other activity that you think your dog might enjoy: nosework (a searching and scenting activity), barn hunt (a searching and finding activity), dock diving (a jumping for distance competition), and so on. On nights when you don't have class, try to spend five to ten minutes practicing some homework or teaching a new trick. For many dogs, this can be every bit as tiring as an off-leash run at the park, and it's easy to do inside if the weather is bad.

INVEST IN A FEW PUZZLE TOYS

Every dog, regardless of his energy level, can benefit from getting to use his brain each day. If you're busy, food puzzle toys are a great way to provide some extra mental stimulation for your dog, without having to devote more time to entertaining him. These are interactive toys that are made to dispense food or treats when your dog paws at them, chews on them, pushes them with his nose, or performs some other action. The best method to get the food will vary depending on the toy, so your pup will need to be creative and experiment with different strategies to be successful.

In many cases, you can actually feed your dog his breakfast and dinner from one of these toys, rather than from a bowl. This is much more fun for him and is an easy way to keep him busy for a while doing something productive.

Stop by your local pet store, or do a quick search online to see lots of examples of puzzle toys. Chances are, you can easily find one (or a few!) that your dog would enjoy.

PLAY AS A RELATIONSHIP BUILDER

For most of us, playing with our dogs comes naturally. They approach life with a sense of fun that's impossible to resist. This is one of the main reasons we have them as companions. What you might not realize, however, is how important play can be in establishing a healthy relationship with your dog.

There is a reason that all intelligent creatures—from wolves to sea otters, horses to dolphins, and lions to grizzly bears—engage in play to some degree. It's theorized that play serves several adaptive purposes, including allowing youngsters to learn how to use their bodies and practice skills they will need for adult life. In highly social species, such as dogs, play also has an important role in cementing relationships.

As humans, most of us can relate to this. We form close relationships with people whose company we enjoy. When we have fun together with our friends, our bond with them grows and deepens.

The same is true for our relationship with our dogs.

Feeding, petting, cuddling, and even training are all ways that we bond with our canine companions, but none of these is quite as powerful, or as pure, as play. When your dog truly enjoys your company and chooses to interact with you for the sheer joy of the game you're playing together, it can feel almost magical.

This, perhaps more than anything else, is the foundation you need to truly be a team—for dog sports, training classes, or just life in general.

If you've never thought much about this before, you're not alone! It's never too late to start, whether you have a new puppy or a much-loved senior dog. Spend some time with your pup today, and pay attention to what he does for fun. Does he like to fetch toys, chase things, or grab and tug when he plays? Notice his preferences, and work with them; whatever he likes, you can find a way to turn it into a game you both enjoy.

Some common forms of play that may work for your dog include:

RETRIEVING TOYS

Many dogs love to chase toys that are thrown for them, and they may or may not naturally bring them back. Experiment with different types of toys to see what your dog likes best: tennis balls, plush toys, Frisbees, and the like.

If he doesn't bring the toy back on his own, you can teach him to do this when you ask (see Six Steps to Fetching Toys in Part II for details). But if he prefers to run around and play keep-away with the toy after he catches it, it's okay to do this too.

TUG-OF-WAR

This is a time-honored game that can be tremendously fun for dogs, especially high-energy working breeds that were bred to grab and bite things. Contrary to what was once believed, playing tug with your dog will not cause aggression or any other problems, so don't worry! Growling is part of the game and is nothing to worry about. To make sure that everyone stays safe, you do want to have a few rules in place:

- Only play tug with your dog's toys, never clothing or other objects.
- If your dog accidentally bites your fingers, the game stops immediately. Just drop the toy and walk away. Your pup will quickly learn that it pays to be careful with his mouth, if he wants to keep playing.
- Teach your dog the "drop it" command (see Six Steps to Training "Drop It" in Part II). This way, you can always get the toy back and put it away if necessary.

CHASE GAMES

Fast movement can be very exciting for some dogs, especially herding breeds and sighthounds. These pups are often sensitive souls who enjoy "noncontact" games more than tugging or roughhousing and may not be highly motivated to retrieve. For this reason, it may take a bit more finesse to find something that they like.

For a dog like this, try running away from him in an open space and encouraging him to chase you. If his eyes light up and he comes darting happily over the grass to follow, you know you're onto something.

Some dogs prefer to always chase you, while others like to take turns being the "chasee" as well. Experiment with both options to see what your dog likes. If he gets excited and wants to bite your hands or clothing when he catches up to you, carry a toy for him to grab instead.

PART II
LIFE SKILLS 101
COMMON ISSUES AND BASIC COMMANDS

Now that you have a basic understanding of how your dog sees the world and the best methods for teaching him what you want, you're ready to move on to specifics!

If you're like most dog owners, you may not have much interest in training your dog's nit-picky behaviors like precision heeling or a formal retrieve. Instead, you want your pup to be able to fit easily into your life without him causing too much trouble. This means teaching him to stop doing things like chewing your furniture or digging holes in the yard (or whatever the unwanted behaviors might be), as well as helping him acquire some simple, practical obedience skills so that you can help him understand the rules.

Every pet parent needs a user-friendly resource to help walk him or her through the normal training issues that come with owning a dog. So if your pup is jumping on guests, snatching food from your countertops, isn't housetrained yet, or has never learned a single obedience command, don't despair: you'll find answers in the pages ahead!

Part II is divided into two main sections. The first section (Easy Solutions for Everyday Problems) deals with problem-solving for various types of "naughty" behavior that are common in pet dogs, while the second section (Obedience Training, One Skill at a Time) provides clear, concise instructions on training each obedience skill that your dog needs to learn in order to be polite and well-mannered.

EASY SOLUTIONS FOR EVERYDAY PROBLEMS

In this section we'll be delving into some of the most common training problems and nuisance behaviors that dog owners run into. Whatever your dog might be doing to embarrass you or make your life difficult, rest assured that you're not alone!

Since dogs don't come to us with an innate understanding of human rules, they often get into trouble simply by being dogs. Without proper direction, your pup is likely to do all kinds of things that come naturally to him, but that you may not appreciate. This could include finding undesirable ways of entertaining himself like chewing or digging, dragging you down the street on walks, irritating your guests by jumping all over them, or even forgetting where to go to the bathroom.

Managing these issues can be overwhelming, especially if you're a fairly new dog owner or if your current pup is a bit more energetic and mischievous than what you're used to. Fortunately, most common behavioral problems can be successfully handled with a combination of smart management and a simple training plan.

Your dog isn't bad, I promise! He just needs to know what you want him to do. We'll discuss each problem separately in the following pages, with practical solutions that you can implement right away.

Housetraining Your Dog

Whether you have a new puppy or a newly adopted adult dog, making sure your pup understands where to eliminate is critically important. Fortunately, housetraining isn't really complicated—it just takes patience and consistency.

To train your dog to go potty outside:

1 ▸ KEEP A REGULAR SCHEDULE

At minimum, most dogs will need to eliminate shortly after each meal as well as when they wake up in the morning or after a nap. Young puppies may need to go out much more frequently than this, as often as every twenty to thirty minutes in some cases. Take your dog out as often as needed to prevent accidents. As he gets more reliable at holding his bladder, you can gradually lengthen the amount of time between trips outside.

2 ▸ FIND A DESIGNATED AREA

For each potty break, take your dog out on a leash to the area you want him to use. Stay quiet and boring; nothing fun happens until he pees.

3 ▸ REWARD YOUR DOG

As soon as he eliminates, praise your pup and reward him with a tasty treat. This is important, because you want your dog to be very motivated to "go" every time you take him out, even if he doesn't really need to. This gives him lots of practice using the correct bathroom area and also makes it less likely that he'll need to pee in between potty breaks.

4 ▸ SUPERVISE YOUR DOG

Inside, keep a close eye on your pup at all times. Keep him in the same room with you so that you can watch him, and don't allow yourself to become distracted. When your puppy is awake and moving around, you should have two eyes on him at all times. This can feel like a full-time job at first, but don't worry! It gets easier with time, as your pup becomes more reliable. If he's napping or busily engaged with a chew toy, you can safely do something else as long as you stay aware of where he is.

5 ▸ USE A CRATE

When your dog is home alone, he should be crated to prevent accidents—most dogs will instinctively avoid soiling the area that they sleep in. If you need some help with this, see Seven Steps to Crate Training for more information on how to teach your pup to be comfortable in the crate.

6 ▸ STOP HIM AT THE SQUAT

If you see your dog start to squat or lift his leg, clap your hands or call his name to startle him, then quickly rush him outside so he can finish up. Praise and reward as usual for eliminating in the correct spot, even if you had to help him get there.

7 ▸ CLEAN UP ACCIDENTS

Remember—accidents happen! Even with a consistent schedule and good supervision, your pup will occasionally forget and make a mess in the house. Use a good-quality enzyme cleaner to thoroughly treat any urine spots. This will ensure that there is no trace odor left behind to attract him back to use this area again.

8 ▸ WAIT A WEEK

Once your pup has gone at least a week without any accidents at all, you can gradually start to give him more freedom in the house without supervision. If he forgets and makes a mess, just go back to watching him more closely and taking him out more often for the next few days—then try again.

9 ▸ BE PATIENT, AND DON'T RUSH THE PROCESS

Most puppies are not reliably housetrained until six to eight months of age, or even older. Newly adopted adult dogs may catch on quicker, depending on their previous history, but you should still expect to spend several weeks making sure they understand the rules. Every dog learns at his own pace, just like human babies do.

Curbing Puppy Biting/Mouthing

If you're a new puppy owner, you've probably already noticed that your adorable, furry little darling has incredibly sharp teeth and loves to bite things. He grabs your sleeves and pant legs, pulls your hair, chews your toes when you sit on the couch, and bites your hands whenever you try to pet him.

As frustrating as this is, you need to realize something important: constant biting and mouthing is normal puppy behavior. This is a natural developmental stage for young dogs, just as human toddlers have an insatiable need to grab and touch things. Your pup will grow out of this habit as he gets older, but fortunately, there are some things you can do in the meantime to make things easier.

To manage play biting and mouthing in your puppy:

1 ▸ FIND SOME TOYS YOUR PUPPY LIKES

Make sure that your pup has a variety of different toys to bite and chew on. Most puppies enjoy floppy fabric tug toys to pull or carry around, as well as plush or rubber squeaky toys. Experiment with different shapes and textures to see what he likes best, and always have plenty of options available.

2 ▸ PROVIDE "DOG FRIENDLY" THINGS TO CHEW ON

Your puppy should also have lots of appropriate items to lie down on and chew on quietly, such as rawhide chews, bully sticks, and puzzle toys such as a Kong stuffed with dog treats. This will be especially important between the ages of three to six months, when he's teething.

3 ▶ REDIRECT WHEN YOUR PUP GETS EXCITED

When your puppy gets too excited and bites you during play, redirect him to one of his toys and encourage him to grab it instead. Praise your puppy for engaging with the toy, and reward him by continuing the game. The more he makes a habit of playing with appropriate toys, the less inclined he'll be to try and use your hands or clothing instead.

4 ▶ DON'T ENABLE BAD HABITS

Never encourage your puppy to grab your hands, sleeves, or pant legs during play, no matter how cute it might seem when he's young. If your puppy learns early on that this is a fun game, rough play with lots of biting and grabbing may become a habit that continues into adulthood. Always redirect him to a toy instead.

5 ▶ PET YOUR PUP WHEN HE'S CALM

If your dog grabs or mouths your hands when you try to pet him, calmly stop petting and ignore him until he settles down. At this age, you may have to wait until he's calm and sleepy before you pet or cuddle him—this is perfectly fine. He will develop more self-control as he gets older.

DOG TRAINING TIP

I don't recommend punishment as a way of dealing with biting and mouthing in puppies. Remember that this is normal behavior, not a problem that needs to be fixed.

Correction-based training techniques such as forcefully grabbing your puppy's muzzle, scruffing him, smacking his nose, or spraying him in the face with water are not necessary to curb this behavior. He will grow out of it on his own as he gets older. These methods can frighten your puppy and make him afraid of you in the future, and can even elicit aggression in some cases.

Curbing Destructive Chewing

Puppies and young dogs are notorious for chewing on things they shouldn't. No matter how much you love your dog, there's nothing more frustrating than dealing with constant damage to your walls or furniture, or finding holes in your favorite shoes or clothing.

Most dogs become less inclined to chew on inappropriate items as they get older, so hang in there—things will get better with time! But if you're dealing with a young, enthusiastic chewer right now, there are some simple things you can to do help.

To solve a problem with destructive chewing:

1 ▸ MANAGE THE ENVIRONMENT

If you have a young dog in the house, you'll need to keep your personal items and belongings put away to prevent them from being damaged. Put your shoes in the closet and close the door as soon as you put them away. Be diligent about putting laundry in a hamper or basket out of your pup's reach. Keep purses, backpacks, electronics, and the like off the floor so that your dog isn't tempted to chew them.

2 ▸ USE A SPRAY-ON DETERRENT

For things that can't be put away (like furniture or electrical cords), use a deterrent spray such as Bitter No Chew spray or Bitter Yuck! spray to make them less attractive for chewing. Applying this type of spray to tempting spots like table legs or baseboards should help convince your pup to find something else to gnaw on.

3 ▶ PROVIDE APPROVED ITEMS FOR CHEWING

Puppies and young dogs have an instinctive drive to use their teeth, so make sure they have plenty of good options available to meet this need. Natural products such as rawhides, bully sticks, beef tracheas, or pig ears work well for many dogs. You can also offer puzzle toys such as a Twist 'n Treat stuffed with cookies or spray cheese, or a frozen Kong filled with peanut butter.

Don't be afraid to try several different things to see what your pup likes best. Remember, if his own stuff is tastier and more fun to eat than your belongings, he's much less likely to seek out inappropriate things to chew on. This makes life easier for both of you.

4 ▶ TAKE YOUR DOG FOR A WALK

Tired dogs tend to be calm, settled, and well-behaved. Dogs with too much energy, on the other hand, are much more likely to go looking for trouble. This often translates to chewing on rugs, walls, or furniture. Go for a jog, let your dog run in the woods, or play a quick game of fetch before settling down for quiet time at home.

5 ▶ SUPERVISE YOUR DOG

If you have an overly enthusiastic chewer, he should never be loose in the house unless you're watching him. If your pup starts to gnaw on the coffee table or the couch, interrupt him by clapping your hands or saying his name, and redirect him to one of his own chew items instead. When you're not home, he should be crated to prevent any problems. See Seven Steps to Crate Training for details on how to get your pup comfortable with a crate.

Crate Training

If you're new to owning a dog, the idea of using a crate (or cage) may seem surprising or even cruel—after all, our dogs are supposed to be part of the family. We don't use crates for our children or human family members, so it might feel strange at first to think about using one for your dog.

The truth is, there are lots of good reasons to teach your dog to be comfortable in a crate. After all, dogs are not humans and they are not bothered by confinement in a small space the way that a person might be. In fact, if trained properly, most dogs see their crate as a safe, comfortable place to sleep or spend time during the day.

Crates can be used to safely confine puppies who aren't housetrained yet, and young dogs who might be destructive when left alone. They are also great for keeping your dog safe when riding in the car and can be used as a portable, familiar "safe place" where he can sleep if you're staying in a hotel.

For these reasons, I always recommend crate training for puppies and newly adopted dogs. Even if you don't use the crate very much on a day-to-day basis, there will always be times when it comes in handy.

To teach your dog to be comfortable in a crate:

1 ▸ CHOOSE THE RIGHT SIZE

Your dog should have enough room in his crate to stand up and turn around, and lie comfortably on his side if he chooses. If he has to duck his head to fit or can't stretch out to sleep, the crate is too small—try the next size up.

2 ▸ LET YOUR DOG EXPLORE

Start by leaving the crate door open so your dog can investigate it at his own pace. Try tossing treats inside when he isn't looking, so he can discover that the crate is very rewarding to explore. If you place a comfy blanket or dog bed in the crate, he may even choose to go in for a nap on his own.

3 ▸ INTRODUCE THE COMMAND

Once your dog is comfortable going in and out of the crate by himself, you can introduce the "kennel up" command. Get your dog's attention, point to the crate, and say, "Kennel up." Toss a treat inside—your dog should go right in after the treat, with no hesitation. Praise and feed him several more treats when he is inside the crate. Keep the door open for now, so he doesn't feel trapped.

4 ▸ CLOSE THE CRATE DOOR

Repeat step 3 several times, until your dog is happily running into the crate and waiting expectantly for his reward as soon as you say, "Kennel up." Close and latch the door, then praise your dog and feed him several treats in a row through the bars. Open the door and let him out again.

5 ▸ START BUILDING DURATION

Once he's comfortable with step 4, you can begin closing the door and leaving him in the crate for short periods. At first, just a few seconds will do, but then slowly work up to five to ten minutes as long as he's comfortable. You can sit nearby on the couch or walk around the room, but stay close by for now so that he doesn't become anxious. Drop a treat into the crate every now and then to reward him for waiting patiently.

6 ▸ WORK UP TO LONGER PERIODS

At this stage, you can begin leaving your pup in the crate a bit longer. When you crate him for more than five to ten minutes, always leave him with a special, long-lasting treat (like a Kong or bully stick) so that he has something to keep him busy. This will help to prevent him from becoming distressed, and it also helps him create a positive association with being in his crate over time. You want him to think that hanging out in his crate equals great things!

7 ▸ USE THE CRATE AS NEEDED

When your dog is comfortable and happy in his crate, you can use it however you choose: during the day when you're not home, at night when you're sleeping, or just for traveling and car trips if you prefer.

SEVEN STEPS TO

Stop Your Dog from Jumping on People

If you have a friendly dog, you probably spend a lot of time trying to keep him from knocking people over when he wants to say hi. This is a very common problem, so don't worry—there's nothing wrong with your dog at all. Wanting to jump up to say hello is very normal, especially if your pup is excited about meeting someone new.

Of course, most of us would prefer that our dogs not do this. Jumping on people is annoying at best, and can be dangerous with large, strong dogs, especially when greeting children or elderly people. Resolving this problem will take some work (and lots of consistency!) on your part, but it's well worth the effort to have a well-mannered dog who can say hello politely.

To teach your dog to greet people without jumping:

1 ▸ AT FIRST, MAKE THINGS EASY

Start with your dog on-leash and in a fairly quiet environment. You will need a helper for the first several training sessions; this can be a member of your household who your dog already knows, if needed. We'll work up to real strangers later on.

2 ▸ ASK YOUR DOG TO SIT

Your helper should approach you and your dog from the front and casually walk past. The helper should not look at your dog or speak to him, and your dog should remain sitting. Use a treat in front of your dog's nose, if needed, to help keep him focused. Praise and reward with a treat once the helper has passed by.

3 ▸ PRACTICE SITTING STILL

Repeat step 2 several times, until your dog is able to sit still without any difficulty as your helper walks by. Remember to praise and reward each time—sitting still is challenging for friendly dogs.

4 ▸ TRY A QUICK TOUCH

This time, ask your helper to briefly touch your dog as he or she walks past. Praise and reward if he holds his sit. If not, just go back to step 2 and practice a bit more, then try again.

5 ▸ WORK UP TO MORE PETTING

Your helper can slowly progress from a brief touch to a pat on the head or a scratch on the chest until, eventually, she or he can stop and say hello to your dog, pet him, and chat briefly with you just like a "real" stranger would do. Praise and reward your dog every time for holding his sit.

6 ▸ REPEAT WITH SOMEONE NEW

When your dog can do steps 1 through 5 perfectly with your original helper, repeat the process with someone else. You may need to practice with several different people before your dog is able to hold his sit successfully while meeting a brand new stranger. This is normal, especially for young or excitable dogs.

7 ▸ TRY A REAL-LIFE GREETING

Once your dog is no longer making any mistakes in training, you're ready to try out his new polite greeting behavior in real life. Remember that this will be harder for him than practicing with someone he knows, so use lots of treats at first to help him be successful. If he gets too excited and stands up or tries to jump, just back up a few paces to help him calm down, remind him to sit, and try again.

FOUR STEPS TO
Stop Counter Surfing

Most dogs are shameless opportunists and will happily snatch unattended food from a table or countertop if they get a chance. This is absolutely normal behavior that is very annoying for us, as humans. If you have a medium- to large-sized dog who can easily reach things in the kitchen, so-called counter surfing can be a real problem.

A combination of management and training is the best way to address this issue. With a few changes to your daily routine and a few quick training sessions, you can stop losing your dinner to an adventurous dog every time you turn your back.

To solve a problem with counter surfing:

1 ▸ PUT AWAY FOOD

Between mealtimes, keep all food in cabinets, pantries, or refrigerators. I know, this is easier said than done, but it's a critical part of breaking your dog's bad habit. Every time he successfully grabs something tasty from your countertop, he's being rewarded for this behavior, which makes it much more difficult to change in the long run.

2 ▸ TEACH YOUR DOG TO "LEAVE IT"

Practice the "leave it" command with food on the counter (detailed instructions for teaching this skill are in Nine Steps to Training "Leave It," later in this part). Keep him on-leash at first to avoid any accidental self-rewarding. When he's good at this during training sessions, say, "Leave it" if you see him eyeing something tasty in the kitchen while you're making dinner. Make sure to praise and reward with a treat when he does what you ask.

3 ▸ PREVENT PROBLEMS WITH A BARRIER

Use a baby gate or something similar to keep your dog out of the kitchen when food is being prepared. This allows you to concentrate on making dinner and keeps your dog out of trouble—a win-win for both of you! You can give him a puzzle toy or something to chew on to help keep him occupied, if needed.

4 ▸ SEND YOUR DOG TO BED

Alternatively, teach your dog the "go to bed" command (see Nine Steps to Training "Go to Bed" later in this part if you need some guidance). Give him a designated mat or dog bed in a corner of the kitchen, and reward him with an occasional treat for staying in his spot. This gives your dog a way to earn tasty treats with good behavior and keeps him from being underfoot when you're busy cooking.

Stop Pulling on the Leash

Taking your dog for a walk should be a pleasant experience for both of you. But if he pulls like a freight train every time you leave the house, it can be hard to enjoy your quality time together. It can also be a safety issue, especially if your pup is large and strong.

Whether your dog is a young puppy who's just learning leash manners or an older dog with a long history of dragging you down the street, there are lots of things you can do to make your walks more manageable.

To help discourage your dog from pulling on the leash:

1 ▸ CHANGE YOUR EQUIPMENT

If your dog normally wears a flat buckle collar or a regular "rear clip" body harness for walks, you may want to consider trying something different. Both of these can inadvertently encourage your dog to pull, since he can lean his body weight into the harness or collar and drive forward if he wants to get somewhere.

Instead, try a head halter (such as a Gentle Leader or Halti) for leash walks. These include a loop that goes over your dog's nose with an attachment point for the leash under the chin, just like a halter for a horse. Head halters are not painful for the dog and do not put any pressure on the throat; they simply make it difficult for your dog to get much leverage to pull, since you have control of his head.

A front-clip harness (such as the Easy Walk Harness) can also be a great choice if your dog has a pulling problem. These work very differently than a traditional harness; because the leash attaches in front, on the chest, they are very effective at redirecting your dog's forward motion and preventing him from being able to pull you.

2 ▸ WHEN YOUR DOG PULLS, STOP WALKING

This might seem simple, but it's important! Remember that dogs do what works: they pull because they're excited, and they want to get where they're going more quickly. As long as this is effective at making you speed up, they'll keep doing it.

As soon as your dog hits the end of the leash and starts to pull, stop in your tracks and wait. When he turns back to look at you and releases tension on the leash, praise him and start walking again.

If you're consistent about this, your pup will learn that keeping the leash loose is the most effective way to keep moving forward. This way, you both get what you want.

3 ▸ REWARD FOR STAYING BESIDE YOU

Teaching your dog what you *do* want is just as important as discouraging him from pulling (see Eight Steps to Training Loose-Leash Walking later in this part for more information on how to train for this skill). With practice, he'll eventually learn to walk beside you without being asked.

Remember to carry treats in your pocket when you take your pup for a walk. Use the treats to reward him for staying with you and walking nicely.

Stop Digging

It's a fact of life that many dogs enjoy digging holes. This is an especially common problem in dogs that were originally bred for hunting and burrowing after rodents, such as dachshunds and terrier breeds. However, digging can be an issue for any dog, especially if he's bored or under-exercised.

So if your dog is in the process of relandscaping your yard, don't worry. This behavior is usually fairly easy to curb with a few simple management changes.

To teach your dog to stop digging holes outside:

1 ▸ GO OUT WITH YOUR DOG

Limit your dog's time in the yard unless you are outside to supervise him. Dogs often dig when they're bored or lonely and can't find anything else to do. Go outside with your dog and play fetch or other games instead of turning him out by himself, or let him relax in the house with you instead.

2 ▸ PROVIDE MORE EXERCISE

Give your dog a chance to burn off some energy, especially before putting him out in the yard alone. Take him for a long walk around the neighborhood, or throw a ball for thirty minutes to give him an opportunity to run. If he's already tired when you put him outside, he's more likely to take a nap than dig a new crater in your flowerbed.

3 ▸ INCREASE MENTAL STIMULATION

If you do need to put your dog outside for a few hours by himself, give him something to do—a chew item like a bully stick, rawhide chew, or cow's ear can work very well for many dogs. A puzzle toy like a Kong stuffed with peanut butter or a Kibble Nibble with his breakfast or dinner inside can also be a great way to keep him busy.

4 ▸ USE BARRIERS TO PREVENT PROBLEMS

If there are specific parts of the yard that your dog tends to dig in or areas that you want him to stay out of such as gardens or flowerbeds, fence off these areas using chicken wire or lattice panels to keep him out.

5 ▸ PROVIDE AN APPROVED DIGGING AREA

If your pup is a committed digger who truly enjoys this activity (rather than a dog who digs only when he's bored or hasn't had enough exercise), consider giving him a designated area to dig in rather than trying to stop this behavior completely. A child's sandbox or a kiddie pool filled with sand or dirt can work very well for this. Bury some of your dog's toys in his digging spot, and encourage him to root around and dig them out. This can be a great way of channeling his drive to dig into something appropriate.

Stop Urine Marking

Whether you're in your own home, visiting friends, or in a public place such as a pet store or training class, there are few things more aggravating than having your dog lift his leg to urinate on something inappropriate. This is an especially common problem for intact males, but neutered males and even females can also urine mark in some cases.

This behavior is driven by normal urges to some extent (especially with intact boys), but can also be prompted by stress or anxiety. It's also more likely to happen in new places or in areas where other dogs have eliminated recently.

To teach your dog to stop urine marking indoors:

1 ▸ ANTICIPATE PROBLEMS BEFORE THEY HAPPEN

Take note of situations that are likely to trigger your dog to lift his leg. Even if your pup doesn't mark indoors at home, be aware that he may be more likely to do this at the vet's office, at the pet store, or even at a friend's house.

2 ▸ SUPERVISE YOUR DOG

Keep a close eye on your pup in places where he is likely to try and mark. If your dog has a history of lifting his leg in inappropriate places, don't let him out of your sight when you're visiting someplace new.

If he's on-leash, pay attention to what he's doing. Don't become distracted with talking or other activities. If he's allowed off-leash, use baby gates or other barriers to keep him in the room with you where you can see him.

3 ▸ WATCH FOR SIGNS OF TROUBLE

Learn to recognize the signs that your dog is about to urinate. Most dogs tend to sniff a particular area with great interest, then turn to align their body with their chosen spot just prior to lifting their leg to pee. Pay attention to your dog's "tells" so that you can anticipate when he's about to try and mark.

4 ▸ INTERRUPT AND REDIRECT

Be ready to interrupt your dog as soon as you see any sign that he's thinking about marking. A simple "Ah-ah," a leash tug, or a hand clap can work well for many dogs. You can also call him back to you for a treat, or you can redirect his attention to a toy or some other activity.

> **DOG TRAINING TIP**
>
> In intact males, neutering often resolves problems with excessive urine marking. Obviously, this isn't an option for show dogs, breeding dogs, or dogs who need to remain intact for medical reasons...but it's something to consider for pet dogs with a penchant for leg-lifting.

5 ▸ TAKE FREQUENT BATHROOM BREAKS

If you know that urine marking can be a problem for your pup, take him outside for frequent potty breaks (about every thirty to sixty minutes) so that he can relieve himself outdoors. It's fine for him to mark on trees, bushes, and clumps of grass—just not inside on walls or furniture.

6 ▸ TRY A BELLY BAND

This is essentially a diaper for male dogs. This device is usually a stretchy band of fabric that goes around the abdomen and covers the penis—you can use an absorbent pad to prevent any leakage, if needed. This may not be ideal for everyday use, but it can be a great option for situations where you can't watch your dog as closely as needed to prevent this activity.

Curb Begging at the Table

You know the look: sad eyes, chin resting on your knee, drool slowly soaking through your pant leg. You know the sound: an excited dog panting heavily beside your dinner plate. If this is a common mealtime occurrence at your house, you're not alone.

Most dog owners know that it's tough to enjoy a meal with their furry friends breathing down their necks the entire time—literally or metaphorically. Dinner guests usually appreciate it even less! Fortunately, with a little foresight and a few quick management changes, this behavior is usually an easy one to fix.

To keep your dog from begging at the dinner table:

1 ▸ NEVER FEED YOUR DOG FROM THE TABLE

Remember that dogs do what works. If sitting next to you, staring soulfully up at your plate is a winning strategy, you can bet that your dog will continue to do it every single night. So if you want to stop this behavior for good, your first step is to stop rewarding it.

Giving your dog a bite of your dinner when you're done is perfectly fine. Just don't do it at the table. Take the goodies to his bowl once dinner is finished and feed him there instead.

2 ▸ USE A BARRIER TO BLOCK ACCESS

Use a baby gate to keep your dog out of the kitchen or dining room while your family eats. Your goal is to prevent accidental "rewards" for begging if someone drops a bite of supper, which can be especially challenging if you have young children.

If your dog barks or whines when he's kept away from the table, give him something else to do. Feed him his own dinner out of a puzzle toy while the family eats, or let him enjoy a special chewy treat like a bully stick or a pig ear.

3 ▸ TEACH THE "GO TO BED" COMMAND

If you want your dog to be able to stay in the room with you while you eat, teach him to "go to bed" on cue (for guidance on this see Nine Steps to Training "Go to Bed" later in this part). Place his mat or dog bed in a designated spot in the dining room, and ask him to stay there while you eat. You can toss him an occasional treat during the meal as long as he's staying quietly in his place. If he gets up, just remind him to go back to his spot—and never feed him while approaching the table. This way, he can still be nearby during dinner, just not drooling on your lap or breathing on your food.

FIVE STEPS TO
Stop Submissive Urination

If you've ever had a dog who is a submissive wetter, then you know what a frustrating problem this can be. Dogs with this issue tend to urinate when they're excited or if they feel anxious or nervous for some reason. Some common situations that may trigger an accidental "pee" include greeting visitors, getting excited when owners come home, or being scolded or punished.

Fortunately, the majority of puppies with submissive urination issues will grow out of this behavior as they get older. Adult dogs of some breeds may have genetic predisposition to this problem, but even with older dogs, training and management can help.

To successfully manage a problem with submissive urination:

1 ▶ DON'T LEAN OVER

Avoid leaning over your dog when petting or greeting him. This posture can be intimidating for many dogs, which often prompts a submissive pee. Instead, crouch down a few feet away to say hello and let him come to you. This puts you on the same level with your dog, meaning that you won't be looming over him in a scary way. Avoiding eye contact during greetings and speaking softly can also be helpful.

2 ▶ TEACH YOUR DOG HOW TO GREET

Train your dog to do something specific when saying hello, such as sitting (see Seven Steps to Stop Your Dog from Jumping on People earlier in this part for more information on how to do this). The process for teaching a dog how to greet is the same, even if your dog has issues with urination rather than jumping up. Having a specific task to focus on can be incredibly helpful for many dogs with this problem and can also help to build your dog's confidence with saying hi if he's a bit anxious or worried.

3 ▸ TAKE A PREEMPTIVE POTTY BREAK

Take your dog outside so that he relieves himself just before visitors arrive. Having an empty bladder means that there won't be a mess to clean up, even if he gets excited about greeting everyone.

Alternatively, take your dog outside on-leash and let him say hello to everyone there. This way, if he does pee, it won't matter. Once he's over the initial excitement, you can all go back inside together.

4 ▸ DON'T PUNISH

Never punish your dog for having an excited "accident," no matter how frustrated you are. Remember that he isn't doing it on purpose—submissive urination is an involuntary reaction to feeling excited or worried, so it's not something he can control. Scolding him will only make him more anxious, which will make the problem worse.

5 ▸ TRY A BELLY BAND

If the problem is severe, consider a diaper or belly band when visitors come over. In most cases, you can remove this once the initial excitement has died down. While it may not be ideal, this option can help prevent messes in the house, which in turn can avoid a lot of aggravation for everyone involved.

FIVE STEPS TO
Curb Excessive Barking

Yes, dogs bark—we all know that this is an unavoidable part of life with our canine companions. They bark to warn us when the mailman comes, to show excitement during play, and even to welcome us when we come home. Most of us consider a certain amount of barking to be normal and take it in stride.

So when does barking cross the line and become a problem that needs to be addressed? Perhaps your dog barks obsessively at every sound outside. Or perhaps he barks at you when he's bored and wants attention, or maybe he gets excited (and noisy!) when visitors come.

Whatever the underlying reason, life with a dog who barks constantly can be difficult. Fortunately, there are some simple things you can do to curb this behavior and give your long-suffering ears a rest.

To help your pup learn to quiet down:

1 ▸ IDENTIFY TRIGGERS

Does your dog alert-bark at things he sees or hears outside? Or is the barking more likely to happen when you get home from work or when your friends stop by to visit? If you can predict when your dog is likely be noisy, you can make some easy changes to your daily routine to help avoid problems.

2 ▸ MANAGE THE ENVIRONMENT

If he barks at things he sees or hears outside, for example, use a white noise machine or decorative window film to help block these things out. Your dog will be much more relaxed, and so will you.

3 ▸ DISTRACT AND REDIRECT

By redirecting your dog's energy to some other activity when he starts to get wound up, you can prevent a lot of excited barking. Toss a handful of kibble on the floor when you get home from work or encourage him to grab a toy and carry it around when visitors stop by. These strategies can help to keep him occupied until the excitement level has died down a bit and he's able to say hello more calmly.

4 ▸ TEACH THE "QUIET" COMMAND

To train this cue, wait until he starts to bark at something and then grab a handful of treats. Say, "Buddy, quiet" and immediately reward him as soon as he looks at you. Practice this each time he barks, gradually asking for longer and longer periods of silence before rewarding—first one second, then two, then three, and so on. Eventually, he'll be able to stop barking entirely when you ask.

5 ▸ DON'T PUNISH

"Quick fixes" like shock or citronella bark collars, squirt bottles, or cans of compressed air work by scaring your dog into silence. They may seem to work temporarily, but they don't address the root cause of the barking or help your dog understand what he should do instead. Worse, they can cause a host of behavioral side effects including generalized anxiety, phobias, and even aggression.

DOG TRAINING TIP

In some cases excessive barking can be a symptom of a more severe behavioral issue such as fear aggression, leash reactivity, or separation anxiety. If the suggestions discussed here don't seem to help, or if you have reason to believe that your dog has a more serious issue, please see Part V: Trouble in Paradise—Understanding and Addressing Behavioral Problems for a more detailed discussion of how these problems can be treated.

FIVE STEPS TO
Stop Car Chasing

For some dogs, the sight of a car driving by is almost impossible to resist; they can't help but try and go after it. This is especially true for herding breeds and other motion-sensitive dogs who were bred to notice and chase down fast-moving things. While this impulse might be understandable, car chasing is an incredibly dangerous behavior. On walks, a dog who lunges after cars can easily become tangled in the leash or even pull his owner into the street. And if your dog is loose and takes off after a car, he could be injured or even killed.

Fortunately, in most cases you can dramatically improve this behavior with careful management and a good training plan.

To help your dog learn not to chase cars:

1 ▸ START WITH LOTS OF DISTANCE

Stand a long way back from the road with your dog on-leash. Make sure you have a good supply of high-value treats in your pocket—cheese, lunch meat, or hot dog slices usually work best for this exercise.

Ideally, you want to be far enough away that your dog is able to notice cars driving by without immediately lunging after them. If this isn't the case, you're too close. You may need to be creative in finding places to train where you're able to get enough distance.

2 ▸ REWARD FOR CALM BEHAVIOR

Each time a car passes by, praise and reward your dog for standing calmly. If he lunges or tries to chase it, just move farther away from the road.

3 ▶ WAIT FOR THE "CHECK IN"

As he gets the hang of things, your dog should start to look expectantly at you for his treat every time a car drives by; this is exactly what you want. Praise and reward him for "checking in" with you, rather than attempting to chase the car.

4 ▶ MOVE CLOSER

Once your dog is doing this easily every time a car passes, you can begin to move closer to the road. Take this training exercise slowly, one step at a time. Continue to reward with a treat every time he looks away from the car and checks in with you instead.

5 ▶ PRACTICE ON THE SIDEWALK

Eventually, your pup should be comfortable standing calmly on the sidewalk with cars driving by only a few feet away. If he gets overly excited or forgets to look at you, just back up a bit to help him calm down and try again.

You may need to carry treats with you on your walks every day to continue rewarding him, even after this new skill is trained—if so, that's okay. For many dogs, car chasing is a very hard-wired behavior that's difficult for them to control. There's nothing wrong with continuing to reward your pup for making the right choice, if he needs this to stay reliable.

DOG TRAINING TIP

Car chasing is a very self-rewarding behavior for most dogs, and one that is difficult to completely eliminate through training. If your dog has a tendency to chase cars, he should never be allowed to run loose in an area with access to the road, no matter how much training you've done. Use a physical barrier such as a fence to keep him safe, or keep him on-leash if needed. Even if he's been a model student, it's not worth the risk.

FOUR STEPS TO
Curb Mounting Dogs or People

Of all the "doggy" things our dogs do, there is perhaps nothing quite so embarrassing for most dog owners as this. Mounting (or humping, as it's sometimes called) is usually related to excitement or frustration and can be directed at other dogs or humans depending on the situation.

Some dogs also do this as a way of initiating play with other dogs, although it may not always be appreciated by their playmates.

To manage a problem with mounting:

1 ▸ SEE IF YOU NEED TO INTERVENE

If your dog occasionally mounts other dogs during play, his playmates may manage things on their own by growling or snapping at him. This is how dogs communicate with each other, and it can be completely normal. If he gets the message and backs off, great! No need for you to get involved.

Some dogs also like to mount inanimate objects such as a stuffed toy or dog bed. This is a self-soothing behavior in some cases, similar to a young child sucking his or her thumb. As long as your dog doesn't do it excessively (to the point of being unable to engage in other activities, or if it causes redness or irritation of the penis in males), this can be perfectly normal also and does not necessarily need any intervention.

2 ▸ LOWER THE EXCITEMENT LEVEL

Since most dogs mount because they are frustrated or overly excited, calming things down a bit will often resolve the problem. If your dog is in a play group with other dogs, call him back to you for a treat and brief rest period to help him settle down—then release him back to play again once he's calmer.

3 ▸ REDIRECT TO SOMETHING ELSE

If your dog gets excited and tries to mount your leg, or if he does this to visitors when they come over, give him something else to do instead. Ask him to "sit" or "down," and reward him with a treat when he complies. You could also encourage him to grab a toy when he gets excited—many dogs are happy to do this as an alternative to mounting.

If he immediately tries to go back to mounting after being briefly redirected, keep him busy with something else for a while to help him settle down. Give him a chew item such as a bully stick or a Kong toy stuffed with peanut butter, or ask him to "go to bed" if he knows this command. Once he's calmer and more relaxed, he should be able to join in normal activities again.

4 ▸ CONSIDER NEUTERING

If your dog is an intact male, consider having him "fixed." Hormones in intact males can make them more prone to mount other dogs and people. While neutering your dog may not completely eliminate this behavior, in many cases you will see a significant reduction in his desire to mount.

OBEDIENCE TRAINING, ONE SKILL AT A TIME

We all know that our dogs need to know some basic things in order to be well-mannered companions, but if you don't have much experience with dog training, it can be hard to know where to start.

You may be intimidated by the idea of trying to teach your dog something new. Maybe Buddy already knows the basics, but you've struggled with teaching him anything beyond a simple "sit" or "down." Or perhaps he's a new puppy or recently adopted adult dog with no prior training—a blank slate of joyful enthusiasm with no manners at all.

Whatever his or your background might be, you'll find help in the following section. Each basic obedience skill is broken down into a simple, step-by-step plan that's concise and easy to follow. You can start at the beginning and work your way through each command in the order they're presented, or you can skip to a specific skill that you're having trouble with—whatever you prefer is fine.

Regardless of how you choose to approach it, you and your dog should be making noticeable progress in no time.

Training Attention: The Name Game

Getting your dog's attention on cue is a vital part of basic obedience training. If you can't get his attention when you need to, it doesn't matter what other skills he might have—he'll be too busy with other things to listen.

For most dog owners, the easiest way to put attention on cue is to teach your dog to look at you automatically whenever you say his name. This is a great game to play with a new puppy (or a newly adopted adult dog) before introducing any other commands.

To teach your dog to respond to his name:

1 ▸ CHOOSE A PLACE TO START

A quiet indoor area, like your living room or kitchen, will probably work best. Keep some tasty treats in your pocket or on a table within easy reach so that you can grab them quickly when you need to.

2 ▸ BE QUIET AND BORING

Wait until your dog isn't looking at you; he might be sniffing the floor or looking out the window. Make sure not to talk to him or play with him. The goal is to be as boring as possible for now. If he's staring at you because he smells the treats, just be patient—he will lose interest and wander off to do something else eventually.

3 ▸ CALL HIS NAME

Say your pup's name in a happy voice: "Buddy!" Odds are, he'll turn to look at you since there's not much else going on. As soon as he does, reward him with a treat.

4 ▸ REWARD EVERY TIME

Repeat this several times, until he is turning immediately to look at you as soon as he hears his name. He should look excited and eager, since he's expecting his treat. Praise and reward every time he listens.

5 ▸ PRACTICE IN NEW PLACES

Once he's good at this indoors, try calling his name in other places: outside on walks, at the pet store, or in the park. You can also start to practice with more distractions, such as when he's barking at something outside the window

DOG TRAINING TIP

Eventually, when your dog has learned some other obedience skills, you can start to use his name to get his attention prior to giving another command. For example, "Buddy, sit" or "Buddy, down." It helps if he's always looking at you expectantly before you ask him to do anything else. Otherwise, he may not respond to your commands simply because he doesn't hear them.

or playing with another dog. These situations are much harder, so make sure to praise and reward enthusiastically when he turns to look at you.

Introducing the Leash

If you have a new puppy (or an adult dog) who has never been taken for walks before, the leash can be a scary thing at first. Dogs don't lead each other around by the neck, so they have no intuitive understanding of what we're trying to do when we attach a leash and start walking. So if your pup lies down and won't move when the leash is on, or if he becomes frightened and struggles to get away, don't worry—this is very normal. It is usually easy to work through these issues with a little patience and encouragement.

To introduce the leash to your dog in a positive way:

1 ▶ LET YOUR DOG GET COMFORTABLE

Start by showing the leash to your dog. Allow him to look at it and sniff it as much as he wants. Many dogs are apprehensive at first about being touched by strange objects, so let him investigate it thoroughly before you try to put it on him.

Some dogs will breeze through this step with no issues, which is great. But if your dog seems anxious or hesitant about the leash, spend a few sessions just getting it out, letting him sniff it, and rewarding with lots of praise and treats. Don't move on to the next step until he approaches you happily when you get the leash out—this means that he associates it with good things and is no longer nervous about it.

2 ▶ ATTACH THE LEASH

Clip the leash to your dog's collar. Immediately praise and reward with a treat, then remove the leash.

3 ▸ BUILD YOUR DOG'S CONFIDENCE

Repeat step 2 several times, until your dog is happily allowing you to attach the leash without any signs of fear or anxiety.

4 ▸ TAKE A STEP

Attach the leash, and then encourage your dog to take a single step toward you. Praise and reward as soon as he does.

Many dogs will initially freeze and not want to move when the leash is attached, so spend as much time on this step as you need to. Help him understand that he can still move around when the leash is on, and reward him for coming toward you when you ask.

5 ▸ START WALKING

Now try walking a few steps with your dog on-leash. Use a treat to encourage him to come with you, and be patient if he seems nervous. Keep the leash slack, without any tension; for many dogs, feeling something pull on their neck is very scary at first and will often cause them to stop and brace themselves against it.

6 ▸ KEEP THE LEASH LOOSE

If your dog gets nervous and refuses to move, don't use the leash to pull him—this will only frighten him and cause him to pull back even more. Instead, keep the leash loose and use a treat to encourage him to walk. Praise and reward as soon as he "unfreezes" and moves forward again.

7 ▸ INCREASE YOUR WALKING DISTANCE

Practice on-leash walking several times a day if you can. Try for a few more steps each session. As long as you're patient and stay positive, you should be able to have your pup going for walks like a pro in no time.

Training "Sit"

We all know that sitting is one of the most important foundation skills for every dog to learn. It's a critical building block for other behaviors like "down" and "stay," and sitting is an easy way for your dog to ask for things politely. Fortunately, it's also one of the easiest obedience skills to teach.

To teach your dog to sit:

1 ▸ START WITH YOUR DOG STANDING IN FRONT OF YOU

For medium-sized or large dogs, you should be standing as well. If your dog is smaller (less than 20 pounds or so), you may find it easier to sit or kneel on the floor.

2 ▸ LURE THE NOSE UP

Hold a tasty treat in front of your dog's nose. Slowly move your hand up and back, over his head. As his nose comes up to follow the treat, his rear end should go down. Many dogs will sit right away the first time you try this—if so, great. Praise and give the treat as soon as his rear end touches the ground.

3 ▸ SHAPE THE SIT

If your dog doesn't sit at first, don't worry! Some dogs (especially toy breeds) have a tendency to jump up for the treat or walk backward to follow the lure. If this happens, you can shape the sit more slowly in several steps.

4 ▸ REWARD FOR SMALL MOVEMENTS

To shape the sit more gradually, use the lure to move your dog's nose up slightly, then praise and reward. Repeat this several times. When he can tilt his head back without jumping or moving backward, move the lure slightly farther. When he bends his back legs slightly, praise and reward.

5 ▸ REWARD FOR A COMPLETED SIT

Continue rewarding your dog for looking up and bending the rear legs, until eventually he goes all the way into a sit. When this happens, have a party: enthusiastic praise and lots of treats!

6 ▸ KEEP YOUR DOG SITTING

If your dog tends to pop up again immediately, continue feeding treats rapid-fire, one after another, as long as he stays in position. Once he catches on that good things will happen if he remains sitting, you can begin to ask for longer sits before rewarding.

7 ▸ PRACTICE IN NEW PLACES

Once your dog is sitting nicely in your living room or kitchen, practice in other rooms in the house, outside in the yard, on walks, and elsewhere. Also practice having your dog sit beside you, as well as in front. This will come in handy for teaching other behaviors, such as heeling or loose-leash walking.

DOG TRAINING TIP

Once your dog has mastered this skill, you can easily incorporate it into his daily routine. Ask for a sit before you throw his ball, put his food bowl down, or attach his leash for a walk. If you're consistent with this rule, sitting will become automatic for your dog whenever he wants something. This is an easy way for him to say please.

Training "Down"

Once your dog knows how to sit, you're ready to tackle the "down" command. Having your dog lie down when asked is a useful skill that comes in handy for lots of reasons; it's a comfortable position when you need him to stay put for a few minutes. In addition, it can help him to relax in stressful or exciting situations, and it serves as a jumping off point for a number of fun tricks including crawl, roll over, and play dead.

To teach your dog to lie down:

1 ▸ START WITH A SIT

Begin with your dog in a sitting position in front of you. Have a good supply of treats handy.

2 ▸ LURE THE NOSE DOWN

Using a treat in your hand, slowly lure your dog's nose straight down toward the floor, and then lure the nose forward between his front paws. You'll be making an "L" shape.

3 ▸ REWARD FOR LYING DOWN

If all goes well, your dog should bend his elbows and lie down to follow the treat. Reward as soon as he performs correctly.

4 ▸ CHANGE YOUR LURING MOTION IF NEEDED

Alternatively, some dogs do better if you move the lure back toward their chest, rather than forward between their front paws. Try this if you're having trouble.

5 ▸ SHAPE THE DOWN

This can be a tough skill to teach at first, so if your dog doesn't lie down right away, you can shape the down step by step. Reward at first for lowering the head, then bending the elbows, and so on. If he stands up, take the treat away immediately and start again from a sit. When your dog finally lies all the way down, give him a handful of treats and lots of praise.

6 ▸ STAY HANDS-OFF

As tempting as it may be, resist the urge to press down on your dog's back or shoulders to physically force him down. Even if you are gentle, this can be frightening for many dogs. You want your dog to be relaxed and happy in the down position, rather than tense or defensive.

7 ▸ INTRODUCE THE COMMAND

Once your dog is lying down easily every time you lure his nose to the floor, you can introduce the verbal "down" command. When you have your dog's attention, say, "Down" and then lure his nose down to the floor to prompt him to lie down. Praise and reward, as usual.

8 ▸ FADE OUT THE LURE

With practice, you will see your dog begin to offer the "down" behavior as soon as he hears the verbal cue. At this point, you can start to fade out the food lure and rely only on the verbal "Down." Make sure to praise and reward when he gets it right!

Training "Stand"

Teaching your dog to stand on cue can be handy for lots of reasons. Show dogs and competitive obedience dogs need to learn this skill for the ring, so if you're interested in pursuing any kind of dog sport with your pup, he'll need to have a good "stand" command ready to go.

In everyday life, you can also ask your dog to stand for paw-wiping when his feet are muddy, when he's on the grooming table, when he needs to be brushed, or when he's at the vet's office for a physical exam.

To teach your dog to stand:

1 ▸ START WITH A SIT

Begin with your dog in a sitting position. You can be in front of him or beside him—whichever you prefer.

2 ▸ LURE THE NOSE FORWARD

Hold a treat in front of your dog's nose, at about chin level. Slowly move the treat forward, away from his body; think about pulling his nose forward with the lure, parallel to the floor.

It's important to do this *slowly* and keep your treat hand level with his chin. If your hand is too high, your dog will scoot forward and continue sitting. Too low, and he'll probably lie down. You want to stay right in the middle.

3 ▸ REWARD FOR STANDING UP

As you move the treat, your dog should shift his weight forward and stand up—stop moving your hand immediately and let him have the treat. You don't want him to continue walking forward, so make sure to praise and reward as soon as his rear end comes up off the ground. He should be standing still as he eats the treat.

4 ▸ INTRODUCE THE COMMAND

You can introduce the verbal cue for this behavior once your dog is popping up smoothly into a stand every time you lure him forward. Say, "Stand" just before you move your hand to guide him into position. Over time, with practice, he will start to respond to the verbal cue alone.

5 ▸ PRACTICE IN NEW PLACES

Once your dog is good at this behavior in the house, try practicing outside on walks or in new places, such as the park or the groomer's. Most dogs prefer being asked to change positions (and getting a reward for complying) rather than being physically maneuvered, especially if they're nervous or worried. A solid "stand" cue can be a great option for sensitive dogs at the vet's office.

SIX STEPS TO
Training "Stay"

Staying in place until you return is one of the most useful skills you can teach your dog. It can keep him calm while you walk away for a moment or prevent him from wandering off while you tie your shoe or fill out paperwork at the vet's office. This behavior can seem daunting at first, especially if your dog is high-energy, but never fear! With patience and a positive attitude, any dog can learn how to stay put when you ask.

To teach your dog to stay:

1 ▸ START WITH A SIT

Begin with your dog in a sitting position in front of you. Give a verbal command and hand signal—usually an open upright hand in front of the dog, like a stop sign, as you say, "Stay." Reward immediately with a treat, and release him by saying, "Okay!"

In the early stages of teaching this behavior, it's important to reward your dog before he has a chance to get up. Remember that he doesn't know yet what "stay" means. Once he catches on that all he needs to do is stay still, you can begin increasing time and distance.

2 ▸ START BUILDING DURATION

Repeat step 1, but wait a second before rewarding. Repeat again, waiting two seconds before rewarding. Then repeat with three seconds, then four, and so on.

If your dog gets up, don't worry. This is a normal part of the process; he just doesn't understand what you want. Withhold the treat, ask him to sit, and try again. Ask for a shorter stay next time so that he can be successful.

3 ▸ TAKE A STEP BACK

Once your dog can stay for five seconds without moving, you can start to add distance. Give your command and hand signal to stay, as above. Take a step backward with one foot only, then return and reward. If this goes well, repeat this process with a full step backward (both feet), then return and reward.

4 ▸ BUILD DISTANCE

Slowly add more distance until you can go all the way across the room, then return and reward.

5 ▸ REWARD IN POSITION

Make sure to always come back to your dog and reward him while he is still sitting, rather than calling him to you or releasing him before you come back. This is important, because dogs are very literal—whatever he is doing at the moment he gets the treat is what he thinks he's being rewarded for. So make sure to reward him for staying, not for getting up.

DOG TRAINING TIP

Remember to always release your dog with a specific word ("okay") or an action (a hand clap, for example) when you return. This word or action lets him know that it's now okay to get up. If you forget to do this consistently each time, your dog will get into the habit of releasing himself whenever he thinks the stay should be over.

6 ▸ ADD SOME CHALLENGES

As your dog gets better at this, introduce some variations. Try walking away with your back to your dog. Skip, run, or bounce a tennis ball nearby while he stays. If he makes a mistake, just reset and try again. With practice, he should be able to stay no matter what is going on around him.

Training "Wait"

Learning to wait politely at the front door rather than bolting out is an essential skill for all dogs to master—especially large, boisterous ones. An untrained dog at the door can easily knock over visitors, injure your shoulder by pulling you out on-leash, or even run into the street and be hurt.

This command requires your dog to have good impulse control, even when something exciting is happening. Be patient with your dog. Learning this skill is trickier for some pups than others, but every dog can learn polite door manners with a little time and effort.

To teach your dog to wait at the door:

1 ▸ START OUT WITH A LEASH

Begin with your dog on-leash, for safety. Stand just inside your front door.

2 ▸ TOUCH THE DOOR

Ask your dog to sit, and say, "Wait." Reach out and lightly touch the doorknob—just a quick touch, no grasping or turning just yet. Praise and reward your dog for holding his sit.

3 ▸ REPOSITION IF NEEDED

If your dog gets excited and rushes toward the door, withhold the treat and try again. Reposition him, ask him to wait, and touch the doorknob. Praise and reward if he stays in place.

4 ▶ REWARD FOR SITTING CALMLY

Repeat this process several times if needed. Before moving on to the next step, make sure that your dog is confidently holding his sit with no difficulty while you touch the doorknob.

5 ▶ TURN THE DOORKNOB

Ask your dog to wait, then grasp the doorknob and start to turn it. Praise and reward if he holds his sit. If not, reposition him and try again.

6 ▶ OPEN THE DOOR

Repeat step 5, and open the door just a crack. Close it again, and praise and reward your dog if he holds his sit.

7 ▶ MAKE IT HARDER

Repeat, opening the door a bit wider. Work your way up to opening the door all the way, leaving it open for a moment, and then closing it again. Remember to reward your dog for staying put.

8 ▶ RELEASE YOUR DOG

Finally, after opening the door, release your dog by saying, "Okay." Then walk through the door together.

9 ▶ USE THE "WAIT" COMMAND IN DAILY LIFE

You should incorporate your dog's "wait" command into your daily routine. When you take him for a walk, ask him to wait at the door until you release him to go through. You should no longer need to use treats at this point; his reward for waiting is being allowed to go out for his walk. If he forgets and rushes to the door before you release him, just close the door and try again.

10 ▸ TRY OFF-LEASH

If you want to practice the "wait" command off-leash, place a baby gate or exercise pen outside the door for safety at first. Alternatively, you can use a long line attached to your dog's collar as a back-up measure.

DOG TRAINING TIP

You can also use the "wait" command to keep your dog from jumping up on guests at the door or from running outside while your family brings groceries in from the car. Just make sure to work up to these scenarios gradually, and reward frequently while he's learning—staying in place with so many distractions going on is hard work!

Training Loose-Leash Walking

Being able to take your dog for a walk without being dragged down the street (or injuring your shoulder) is one of the most basic goals that most owners strive for. If your dog darts back and forth in front of you, hangs back and doesn't want to walk, or pulls like a freight train, don't despair! Loose-leash walking isn't all that difficult to teach; it just takes patience and consistency.

To teach your dog to walk nicely on-leash:

1 ▸ START WITH A SIT

Begin with your dog sitting beside you. Keep several treats in your hand nearest to the dog—you will use this hand to reward. Hold the leash in your other hand so that it comes across in front of your body. Don't worry. Your treat hand will be keeping the dog in position, not the leash.

2 ▸ GET YOUR DOG'S ATTENTION

Call your dog's name, say, "Let's go," and start walking.

3 ▸ REWARD IMMEDIATELY

Reward your dog with a treat as he gets up to walk with you. Use your treat hand in front of his nose to keep him from forging forward, if necessary.

4 ▶ TRY A FEW STEPS TOGETHER

Walk a few steps, rewarding continuously as long as your dog is beside you and paying attention. When you stop, ask him to sit beside you again—use your treat hand to help guide him if needed.

5 ▶ BUILD DURATION

As your dog gets better at this, start to ask for two steps beside you before rewarding. Then three steps, then four. Keep practicing until he can walk nicely beside you all the way across the room for a single treat.

Keep your treat hand up at your waist when you aren't actively giving a reward. This prevents your dog from becoming excessively fixated or jumping at it. At this stage, you don't want to be leading your dog around with your hand in front of his nose. He should be choosing to walk beside you, with your hand up out of the way.

6 ▶ ADD SOME CHALLENGES

Try practicing in different parts of the house or in a quiet area outside such as a fenced backyard. Add in circles, turns, and changes in speed to make things more fun for both of you.

7 ▶ INCORPORATE INTO DAILY LIFE

When you start to use this skill on real-life walks, make things easy at first. Intersperse short periods of loose-leash walking with attention (a few steps at a time, always rewarding with a treat) with "free time" when your dog is allowed to sniff, pee on bushes, and so on.

8 ▶ PREVENT PULLING

Consistency is important, so consider using a walking aid such as a head collar or no-pull harness to prevent your dog from pulling on the leash while you're teaching this skill. Once he's good at walking nicely with you, you can transition back to a regular buckle collar for walks if you wish.

Training Recall

The recall, or coming when called, is one of the most important skills your dog will ever learn. It may quite literally save his life someday, so it's worth teaching well. More than anything else, the key to a reliable recall is making things fun.

To teach your dog to come when called:

1 ▸ START ON-LEASH

With your dog on-leash, begin walking in a relatively boring environment such as an indoor hallway or a quiet backyard.

2 ▸ CALL FOR YOUR DOG

Allow your dog to get a few feet in front of you. Call your pup's name in a happy voice and give your recall cue ("Buddy, come"). Quickly back up several steps, encouraging your dog to follow and sit in front of you. You can raise your treat hand above your dog's head as he gets close to encourage him to sit—no need to give a separate command. We want the sit to be a built-in part of his recall cue, to ensure that he stays put once he comes. Reward with a tasty treat once he is sitting.

3 ▸ MAKE IT FUN

Repeat step 2 several times until your dog turns immediately, comes to you, and sits in front as soon as he hears the cue. Remember to back up quickly as you call for him. This will help get your dog excited about the game, which ensures a fast and reliable response.

4 ▸ ADD SOME DISTANCE

Start to add more distance once your dog is doing well. If you're work-ing outdoors, use a long line for safety—your pup won't be ready for true off-leash work just yet. Practice calling him from 10 feet away, then 20, then 30. Make sure to run backward so he can chase you, and give him a jackpot of tasty treats as soon as he comes and sits.

5 ▸ TRY IT IN REAL LIFE

Start using your recall cue in real-life scenarios. The goal is for your dog to reliably turn on a dime and come racing toward you from any distance as soon as you call. Try recalling him when he's running loose at the park, playing with other dogs, or if he bolts out the front door without a leash.

6 ▸ REWARD EVERY TIME

Remember to reward your dog with something wonderful every time you recall, even after your recall is trained—an extra-special treat or a quick game of tug or chase are terrific options. Whatever he enjoys the most! This skill is challenging for your dog, especially in dis-tracting environments, so make sure it's always worth his while.

DOG TRAINING TIP

Never recall your dog to punish him or in preparation for something unpleasant like a bath or nail trim—otherwise, you run the risk of teaching him to avoid you when you recall him. Your recall cue should always predict great things. If you need to do something he won't like, go and get him instead. This way, you can save your "come" com-mand for when you really need it.

Training "Leave It"

In the course of your dog's life, he will come across many things that you would probably prefer he not touch. Whether it's a discarded food wrapper on the street, something dead and smelly at the park, or a plate of food on the coffee table in your living room at home, you need a way to ask your dog to back off and leave something alone—even if he's very interested in it!

To teach your dog to leave it:

1 ▶ SET THE STAGE FOR TRAINING

Start out in a quiet, boring environment: indoors or a quiet backyard is best. Place a dog bowl with a few pieces of kibble or a dry Milk-Bone on the floor. Make sure that you have much tastier treats in your pocket or in a training bag at your waist where you can reach them easily.

2 ▶ BRING IN YOUR DOG

Lead your pup into the room (or yard) on-leash. Slowly walk him toward the bowl until he notices it. Most dogs will show interest in approaching the bowl to sniff it, once they smell the food inside.

3 ▶ STAND STILL AND WAIT

As soon as your dog fixates on the bowl, stop. He will likely pull on the leash, ignoring you at first to try and reach the food. This is normal; just wait quietly, keeping your feet planted so that he can't pull you toward the bowl.

4 ▶ REWARD FOR LOOKING AT YOU

Eventually, your dog will realize that straining forward on the leash is not working. At this point, he will become somewhat puzzled and probably will turn back to look at you. As soon as this happens, praise enthusiastically and reward with an extra tasty treat from your pocket.

If your dog doesn't turn back to look at you on his own within thirty to sixty seconds, you can help him by saying his name. Praise and reward as soon as he looks away from the bowl. You shouldn't need to help him more than once or twice before he starts to look back at you on his own.

5 ▶ PRACTICE TO BUILD CONFIDENCE

Take your dog out of the room for a moment, then bring him back in to repeat steps 2–4. Do this a few times, until he barely glances at the bowl before looking eagerly at you for his treat.

6 ▶ INTRODUCE THE COMMAND

At this point, you can introduce the verbal cue for this behavior. As he starts to look at the bowl, say, "Leave it." He should quickly turn away and look at you, just as you've practiced. Praise and reward.

7 ▶ MAKE IT HARDER

Repeat this exercise with progressively more exciting treats in the dog bowl. Try using soft and smelly jerky treats, pieces of cheese, and even hot dog slices.

8 ▶ TRY IT OFF-LEASH

To practice the "leave it" command off-leash, you will need a helper to stand near the food bowl. His or her job is to pick up the bowl immediately if your dog fails to listen so that he doesn't accidentally self-reward by helping himself to the off-limits snacks. Alternatively, you can use a closed container with a lid so that your dog can't actually get to the treats.

9 ▶ USE THE "LEAVE IT" COMMAND IN REAL LIFE

Once your dog has mastered this skill, you can use it on walks, at the park, and around the house—anywhere he might come across something interesting that you don't want him to bother.

Training "Drop It"

All dogs, no matter how well-behaved they may be, occasionally pick up things they shouldn't. Whether your pup likes to grab bits of litter off the sidewalk, steal chicken bones from the garbage can, or play keep-away with your favorite pair of slippers, being able to ask him to drop whatever he has in his mouth is tremendously useful.

To teach your dog to drop it:

1 ▶ CHOOSE A TOY FOR PRACTICE

In the early stages of this training start out with something easy, such as your dog's favorite toy. You'll work your way up to forbidden items later on.

2 ▶ ENCOURAGE YOUR DOG TO GRAB THE TOY

Use the toy to play with your dog. Encourage him to pick it up in his mouth. When he's holding the toy, say, "Drop it" in a cheerful voice and hold a tasty treat in front of his nose.

3 ▶ TRADE FOR A TREAT

Assuming that your treat is tempting enough, he should happily drop the toy. Praise him as soon as he does this, and let him have the treat.

4 ▸ PRACTICE TO BUILD CONFIDENCE

Repeat this several times, until he is eagerly spitting out the toy as soon as you say, "Drop it." Make sure that you still praise and reward with a treat after he has dropped the toy.

5 ▸ TRY MORE CHALLENGING ITEMS

Practice with progressively more difficult items such as a tissue or paper towel, an empty food wrapper, or a rawhide bone. At each step, you want your dog to be relaxed and happy about dropping the object when you ask. If he seems tense or worried, back up and make things easier.

Note: if your dog growls, snaps, or shows other signs of aggression when you try this exercise, stop. See Resource Guarding in Part V for more information on dealing with this problem.

6 ▸ USE "DROP IT" IN REAL LIFE

When your dog is happily dropping whatever you ask during your practice sessions, you can try out his new skills in real life. Carry tasty treats in your pocket when you go for a walk, or keep some handy in the kitchen or living room. If he picks up something he shouldn't have, don't panic—just say, "Drop it" and reward generously when he listens.

SIX STEPS TO
Training "Off"

Teaching your dog to get off of the couch on cue is handy, especially for sensitive dogs who may not like to be physically pushed or pulled onto the floor. You can also use this command to ask your dog to hop down from a comfy chair, your bed, or any other elevated spot where he may be resting.

To teach your dog the "off" command:

1 ▶ FIND AN OPPORTUNITY

Choose a time when your dog is resting on the couch to introduce this skill. Ideally, he should be settled in and comfortable but not asleep.

2 ▶ LURE YOUR DOG OFF WITH A TREAT

Say his name to get his attention, show him a tasty treat, and say, "Off." Use the treat to lure him onto the floor, then praise and reward as soon as he hops off the couch.

3 ▶ RESET FOR ANOTHER TRY

Encourage him to get back on the couch by patting the cushions, and so forth. Once he does, say, "Off" and lure him back onto the floor. Praise and reward as before.

4 ▶ PRACTICE TO BUILD CONFIDENCE

Repeat this sequence several times, provided that your dog is cooperative and enjoying the game. If he gets bored or confused, just wait until later when he's resting on the couch again and then practice some more at that point.

5 ▶ FADE OUT THE LURE

When your dog is hopping down smoothly as soon as he sees the treat, try giving the command on its own first. Say, "Buddy, off" and gesture toward the floor with your hand. Give him a bit of encouragement if you need to. When he hops down, praise enthusiastically and reward with a treat from your pocket.

6 ▶ USE THE "OFF" COMMAND IN REAL LIFE

With practice, your dog should happily jump down off the couch (or your bed or your easy-chair) whenever you ask him to. Using this command is much easier for both of you than trying to force him down!

Training "Touch" (Hand Target)

Teaching your dog to "touch," or bump your outstretched hand with his nose, can be surprisingly useful. It gives you an easy way to move him around without physically pushing him or pulling on his collar. It's also a fun way to redirect his attention when needed. This can be especially handy for working with sensitive dogs.

To teach your dog to touch your hand:

1 ▸ START IN A QUIET ENVIRONMENT

Make sure that you have plenty of tasty treats handy and that you have your dog's attention.

2 ▸ PRESENT YOUR HAND

Hold out your hand toward your dog, palm up, at his nose level.

3 ▸ REWARD FOR SNIFFING

Most dogs will naturally move forward to sniff your hand. As soon as his nose makes contact, say, "Yes" and reward with a treat from your other hand.

The verbal cue, "Yes" is very important—it marks the instant that your dog is doing what you want, which is what he needs know so that he can understand what the reward is for. Good timing is critical.

4 ▸ PRACTICE TO BUILD CONFIDENCE

Repeat this sequence several times. As your dog begins to understand the game, he will begin to bump your hand more confidently
with his nose as soon as you present it.

5 ▸ INTRODUCE THE COMMAND

At this point, you can start to introduce the verbal cue for this behavior. As you present your hand, say, "Touch." Then praise and reward
as before, as soon as he touches your hand.

6 ▸ ADD SOME CHALLENGES

Vary the exercise by holding your hand out to the side of your body,
using the other hand, or even holding your hand higher so that your
dog has to jump to touch it. Make sure to praise and reward every
time he gets it right.

DOG TRAINING TIP

The "touch" command is a fun behavior for both dogs and owners,
and most dogs catch on quickly. Once learned, you can use this skill
in a variety of ways in your daily life:

- Asking your dog to move to a particular place
- Refocusing his attention when he's distracted
- Interrupting unwanted behavior such as barking, jumping, and
  the like

NINE STEPS TO

Training "Go to Bed"

As much as we love our dogs, there are times when we don't want them underfoot. Teaching your dog to stay on his bed can be a great way to make sure he's safely out of the way without having to lock him in a crate or put him in a separate room.

To teach your dog to "go to bed":

1 ▸ CHOOSE A DESIGNATED SPOT

Decide where you want your dog to lie when you ask him to "go to bed." This could be a permanent location such as a piece of furniture or something portable like a dog bed or yoga mat.

2 ▸ LURE YOUR DOG TO HIS PLACE

Show your dog his special "bed" and use a treat to lure him onto it. Praise and feed several treats in a row once he's standing on his bed. Then release him by saying, "Okay." Using gestures like bending over and clapping your hands will help him understand that he's free to leave now.

3 ▸ PRACTICE WITHOUT THE LURE

Repeat step 2 several times, until he's happily getting onto his bed as soon as he sees it without needing you to guide him.

4 ▸ ASK HIM TO LIE DOWN

When he's comfortable getting on the bed in a standing position, tell him to lie down. You can use a treat to lure him down if he doesn't yet know the "down" command. Praise and give several treats in a row once he's lying down on the bed.

5 ▸ PRAISE AND REWARD FOR GETTING IT RIGHT

Repeat step 4 several times. By now, your dog should be eagerly approaching the bed and lying down without any prompting from you. Make sure to praise and reward every time!

6 ▸ INTRODUCE THE "GO TO BED" COMMAND

At this point, you can start to introduce the verbal cue. Point to the bed, and say, "Go to bed." Your dog should happily go to his bed and lie down, just as you've practiced. Give lots of enthusiastic praise and reward with a treat.

7 ▸ START ADDING DURATION

Try standing nearby and giving a treat every few seconds at first, as long as your dog stays in place. Sit on the couch and watch TV, tossing him a treat occasionally. If he gets up, just remind him by saying, "Go to bed." Be sure to reward him for going back to his place.

8 ▸ GIVE HIM SOMETHING TO DO

For longer periods (thirty minutes or more) you can also give your dog something special to chew on. This will help keep him relaxed—a bully stick, rawhide chew, cow or pig ear, or a puzzle toy such as a Kong stuffed with peanut butter are all good options.

9 ▸ USE THE "GO TO BED" COMMAND IN REAL LIFE

With practice, your dog should become very comfortable going to his bed and staying there until you release him. Just make sure to reward frequently at first, especially in distracting situations, until he gets the hang of things.

Fetching Toys

There's nothing like a rousing game of fetch with your canine pal. Most dogs love this game because they get to chase down "prey" (their ball or toy) and bring it back to you for another throw. It's a fun way for both of you to bond, and it's also a great way to exercise your dog without having to do much work yourself.

Some dogs (especially retrieving breeds) will instinctively fetch toys and bring them back to you without any training at all. If you have a dog like this, consider yourself lucky! If not, don't despair—most dogs can learn to fetch toys quite easily, if you teach them how step by step.

To teach your dog to fetch his toy:

1 ▸ CHOOSE A SUITABLE TOY

Begin with a soft plush toy, if you have one. You want it to be large enough for both you and your dog to hold on to at once.

2 ▸ GET YOUR DOG INTERESTED

Wiggle the toy along the ground for your pup to pounce on, or hold it in your hand and let him chase you. You want him to be excited about getting the toy before you throw it.

3 ▸ THROW THE TOY

Toss the toy a short distance—just a couple of feet. As soon as your dog picks it up, praise him and encourage him to play with you. Grab the toy and tug on it, if he likes that. Clap your hands and run backward, encouraging him to run after you. You want him to get in the habit of coming toward you with the toy as soon as he grabs it, so that the two of you can play with it together.

4 ▸ PRACTICE TO BUILD ENTHUSIASM

Repeat step 3 several times. Keep things fun and lighthearted.

5 ▸ ADD MORE DISTANCE

When your dog is eagerly turning back to you with his toy as soon as he picks up it, try tossing it a bit farther. First 5 feet away, then 10, then 20. Make sure to praise your dog and encourage him to come back to you every time.

As you increase the distance, you may find that he drops the toy before getting all the way back to you. If this happens, just go back to shorter distances for a while. Make sure that playing with you is lots of fun when he does bring the toy back—lots of tugging, chasing you with the toy, and the like.

6 ▸ TRY DIFFERENT TOYS

Once your dog has mastered fetch with a plush toy, you can repeat the process with a tennis ball or another toy if you like. Interactive play like tugging is more difficult with a tennis ball, which is why the plush toy is a better option for beginners, but feel free to work up to harder items as your dog's fetching skills improve.

Teaching Hand Signals

If you've used a food lure to train most of your dog's obedience skills, you may find that your dog already knows quite a few hand signals. Dogs are very attuned to our body language—they often learn to recognize the hand and body movements that you use to cue a behavior even before they learn the verbal command.

For basic skills like "sit" or "down," the hand movement that you originally used to guide your dog into position can become an easy hand signal. But what if you want to teach a brand new signal for a behavior your dog already knows? Fortunately, this isn't hard to do.

To add a new hand signal to an existing behavior:

1 ▸ START WITH SOMETHING SIMPLE

Begin with a behavior that your dog knows well. Make sure that he can perform this skill easily in response to a verbal cue, like "Sit" or "Down."

2 ▸ DECIDE ON YOUR NEW HAND SIGNAL

Whatever you choose, it should be something distinct and easy for your dog to see; otherwise, he may get confused or have trouble figuring out what you want. Some commonly used hand signals in obedience competition include a hand raised in the air for "down," a scooping upward movement with an open palm for "sit," and a quick sweeping motion across your body for "come."

You can use whatever you like, as long as you're consistent. Be creative, and choose something that makes sense for you and your dog.

3 ▸ INTRODUCE THE SIGNAL

Give the new hand signal, pause briefly, and then give your verbal command and/or cue the behavior with your normal body language. Praise and reward when your dog complies.

4 ▸ PRACTICE TO BUILD CONFIDENCE

Repeat step 3 several times. It will take a while for your dog to form this new association, so you may need to practice this five to ten times in a row for several separate sessions. Be patient and consistent until he figures it out.

5 ▸ WATCH FOR YOUR DOG TO CATCH ON

With practice, you should notice your dog starting to perform the behavior as soon as you give the hand signal, rather than waiting for the verbal cue or extra prompting—this is exactly what you want. Praise enthusiastically and reward when this happens.

6 ▸ GIVE THE HAND SIGNAL BY ITSELF

If your dog looks puzzled the first time you try this, just wait a few seconds and let him think. If he performs the behavior, immediately praise and reward. If not, go back to step 5 for a few repetitions, then try again.

7 ▸ USE YOUR HAND SIGNAL IN REAL LIFE

Eventually, you should be able to use your new hand signal to cue the behavior without any other prompting. This can come in handy for signaling your dog at a distance, or in situations where you might need to be quiet.

Fading Out the Treats

As you may have noticed, most obedience commands are initially taught by using a food lure in your hand. Luring is great for guiding your dog into position during the early stages of learning a new behavior, and it also makes it easy to reward at the right moment.

But since you don't want to lure your dog with a treat forever, you need a plan for fading out the food lure without losing your dog's interest. It's important to do this carefully step by step to avoid having your pup decide to "tune you out" as soon as the treats are gone.

To fade out the visible food lure for any obedience behavior:

1 ▸ START WITH AN EASY BEHAVIOR

Begin with an obedience skill your dog knows well, such as "sit." We'll use this as our example for now, but you can go through the same process for every command your dog knows.

2 ▸ USE THE LURE TO GET THINGS ROLLING

Ask your dog to sit two or three times in a row, using the food lure as usual. Praise and reward for each correct response. This will help to make sure he knows what to expect when you try it without the treat.

3 ▸ TRY IT WITHOUT THE TREAT

Now pretend that you have a treat in your hand, and "lure" your dog into position with the same hand motion you normally use. Praise and reward with a treat from your other hand as soon as he sits.

4 ▸ PRACTICE TO BUILD CONFIDENCE

Repeat step 3 several times. Make sure that your dog is confidently sitting each time before moving on.

5 ▸ USE AN OPEN HAND

Ask your dog to sit using a flat, open hand in the same motion that you were using before. It should be the same movement, just an obviously empty hand. This is the real test of what your dog understands. If he sits, praise enthusiastically, and then reward with a treat from your pocket or your other hand.

This is an important step. At this stage, you want your dog to learn that he will still get a treat for doing what you ask, even if he doesn't see one beforehand.

6 ▸ KEEP TREATS HANDY TO REWARD

Carry treats in your pocket or keep them easily accessible around the house, so that you can practice asking your dog for simple obedience behaviors throughout the day. Continue to reward with a treat each time for at least two to four weeks to build your dog's confidence and to make sure that listening to you is a solid habit.

7 ▸ TRANSITION TO "LIFE REWARDS"

Eventually, as long as things are going well, you can begin to incorporate obedience skills into daily life without always using treats. Ask him to sit, then attach his leash to go for a walk. Ask for a down before opening the car door at the park, or have him stay while you put his dinner bowl on the floor.

Anything your dog likes can be a reward, so be creative. Just make sure you have a solid foundation first, and don't be afraid to back up and use treats again for a while if he gets confused.

Incorporating Training Into Daily Life

Believe me, I know—finding time each day to work on training can seem like an impossible task. Most of us already have busy lives, with lots of things to accomplish from morning to night. But if you want a well-mannered companion, you also know that training has to be an everyday commitment.

Luckily, achieving this goal isn't nearly as difficult as you might imagine. In fact, you might be surprised to learn that the most effective way to train isn't by spending hours at a time drilling your dog on his obedience skills...it's by incorporating your training practice into normal activities, and finding a few minutes here and there for a quick practice session when needed.

To train your dog as part of your daily routine:

1 ▸ KEEP IT SHORT AND SWEET

Aim for several short training sessions (two to three minutes each) throughout the course of the day. This is often much easier than setting aside a thirty-minute block of time for training, and it is also much more effective. Dogs learn best in short sessions like this, so it's a win-win for both of you.

Grab a handful of treats and practice with your dog during each commercial break of a TV show you're watching, while your morning cup of coffee is brewing, or while the oven is preheating for dinner.

2 ▸ CATCH YOUR DOG OFF GUARD

Surprise your dog several times a day by asking for a behavior he knows—randomly, out of the blue. You can do this on walks, during playtime, or while going about your normal routine in the house. Ask him for a sit or down, or use your "come" command to call him to you. Praise and reward with a treat when he does what you ask.

3 ▸ INCORPORATE OBEDIENCE GAMES INTO NORMAL LIFE

Make a game out of practicing your pup's skills while you do normal, everyday things. For example, ask him to sit and stay while you brush your teeth in the morning. If he can do it, praise and reward. If not, try again later with something else. This helps him learn that listening to you is worth his while, since he never knows when he might get an unexpected chance to earn a treat.

4 ▸ USE YOUR DOG'S SKILLS TO MAKE LIFE EASIER

Remind him to wait at the front door before going outside, or ask for a sit before putting his dinner bowl down. On walks, ask for several steps of polite, attentive loose-leash walking. Then release him to sniff and pee on bushes for a few minutes as a reward.

Ultimately, this is what obedience training is all about: making life easier with your dog! Once he has several skills that he knows well, you can be creative about finding ways to use them around the house every day. This way, he never has a chance to "forget" his training, and you get to reap the benefits of a polite, cooperative companion who does what you ask.

EIGHT STEPS TO
Adding Distractions

When you're first teaching a new behavior, it's important to start in a quiet area without much else going on. Dogs, like people, learn much better when they can concentrate. But as we all know, the world is full of distractions. This can make things much more challenging when you're ready to start using your dog's obedience skills in real life, especially if he's very social or has a short attention span.

The good news is, your pup can learn to focus and pay attention even when there are exciting things happening nearby; you just need to teach him how.

To teach your dog to focus in the presence of distractions:

1 ▸ START WITH SOMETHING SIMPLE

Begin with a few skills your dog knows well, like sit, down, and stay. Don't try to add distractions for behaviors that he's still learning—this will only confuse him and make things more difficult.

2 ▸ DO SOME "WARM-UP" REPETITIONS

Let your dog do a few practice reps while everything is quiet to make sure that you have his attention and he knows what to do.

3 ▸ BRING IN SOMETHING NEW

Begin introducing various types of distractions to the environment, one at a time. Start with easy changes and work your way up to more difficult challenges. With each new added wrinkle, praise and reward him for listening to you and doing what you ask.

4 ▸ SEE IF YOUR PUP CAN SIT, DOWN, STAY, ETC.

Try the following:

- **Noisy distractions**
  - Music playing on the radio
  - Kids laughing and playing outside
  - Dogs barking in the distance
- **Visual distractions**
  - Cars passing on the street
  - A dog walking by outside the window
  - People looking at him from a distance
- **Social distractions**
  - A family member talking to him
  - A stranger walking by a few feet away
  - Visitors coming into the house

5 ▸ REWARD FOR SUCCESS

Remember to praise and reward your dog generously each time he stays focused and chooses to ignore something tempting that is going on nearby. This is a hard skill for most dogs, and some will need to progress more slowly than others.

6 ▸ DON'T PUNISH FOR MISTAKES

If your dog gets distracted or confused, that's okay. Don't scold him. Just try something a bit easier next time, and work your way back up to the harder challenges.

Your goal with distraction training is *not* to trick your dog into making a mistake so that you can scold him. This is unfair, and it is counterproductive in the long run. Instead, increase the difficulty of your distractions gradually so that he can be successful.

7 ▸ ADD SOME EXTRA CHALLENGES

When your dog is breezing through the previous scenarios with no problems, try these "extra credit" challenges to really test his focus:

- While your dog is working with you, have a helper crouch down and talk to him from a distance, encouraging him to come over and say hello instead of staying with you.
- Ask a family member to "accidentally" drop a piece of tasty food nearby. Just make sure they're ready to pick it up quickly if your pup decides to try and grab it.
- Get a friend to bounce a tennis ball nearby or dangle a toy temptingly from their hand as they walk past.

8 ▸ USE YOUR DOG'S SKILLS IN REAL LIFE

With practice, your pup will eventually learn to stay happily focused on you no matter what else is happening around him. This is a vital part of real-life obedience, so it pays to teach it well.

Transferring Skills to New Environments

"But he always does it at home!"

This is a common refrain in most beginner obedience classes, as many struggling dog owners can't understand why their pup has seemingly forgotten everything he knows. It might surprise you to know that this is completely normal. Dogs are quick learners and very smart in some ways, but they're not very good at transferring skills they've learned to new places.

This means that even though your pup might be an obedience rock star in your living room at home, at the park he might stare blankly at you when you ask him to sit or lie down. If he's never practiced those skills there, he's not being stubborn or disobedient—he truly doesn't understand what you mean.

Fortunately, this problem can be overcome with a bit of extra time and effort. The more new places you can take your dog for practice, the easier it will be for him to understand that the "sit" command always means the same thing, whether it's at the vet's office, in a training class, or while shopping at the pet store.

To help your dog generalize his obedience skills to new places:

1 ▸ START WITH SOMETHING SIMPLE

Begin with easy behaviors that your dog knows well, especially in the beginning. Later on, as your dog becomes more experienced, he'll be able to handle learning new things in different places. But for now, keep it simple. Focus on fun tricks or basic obedience skills that he's already good at.

2 ▸ TRY DIFFERENT ROOMS INDOORS

Practice these skills in every room in your house. If you do most of your training in the living room, your pup may be totally baffled the first time you try working in the bedroom. Aim to do a two- to three-minute training session in a different room every day—the kitchen, the basement, your home office, even in the hallway.

3 ▸ MOVE OUTSIDE

Do a training session in the front yard, in the backyard, on the patio, or on the deck. Each of these locations will feel different to your dog, so be patient if he gets confused. Make sure to use lots of praise and rewards, and help him out by luring with a treat if he needs to be reminded of what to do.

4 ▸ TAKE IT ON THE ROAD

When your dog can do any behavior you ask, no matter where he is in the house (or outside in your yard), you're ready to take things to the next level. You don't necessarily have to go far for an effective practice session. Walk down the block, and do a quick two- to three-minute session in a neighbor's yard. Practice in the field at the end of your street or at the neighborhood playground.

Other good places to take your dog for training practice include city parks, pet shops, and hardware stores such as Lowe's or The Home Depot. You can also go to public places like grocery stores or banks and practice in the parking lot outside.

5 ▸ KEEP UP THE GOOD WORK

The more places you're able to practice, the easier everything will be. Eventually, your dog should be able to show off all of his obedience skills perfectly on the first try, in a brand new place. So be patient and keep searching out new spots for training. Make a game of this, and your pup will enjoy it too.

Going Off-Leash

Now that your dog has some basic skills under his belt, you may be wondering when you can take off the training wheels and give things a try without the leash. This is a big milestone, so congratulations! As a dog owner, there are few things more satisfying than being able to trust your canine buddy to be off-leash beside you without running away.

Like everything else in training, though, transitioning to off-leash obedience takes patience and a carefully thought-out plan. If you try it before your pup is ready, you may set back your training...or worse, end up with a lost or injured dog. So do your dog (and yourself) a favor and make sure you're setting him up for success.

To introduce your dog to off-leash obedience:

1 ▸ CHOOSE YOUR ENVIRONMENT

Start with your dog on-leash in a boring, fully enclosed area such as your garage or basement. Bring an ample supply of high-value food treats. You'll need them to ensure that you're more interesting than anything else once the leash is off.

2 ▸ TAKE OFF THE LEASH

Remove the leash and immediately praise and reward your dog. This might feel strange at first, but it's an important step. You want your dog to get into the habit of looking at you expectantly for his treat when the leash is unclipped, rather than heading for the hills. Later on, you can work up to asking him to do something first, but for now just give him the treat for free.

3 ▸ GIVE AN EASY COMMAND

Ask your dog for a few quick obedience behaviors that he knows well, such as sit, down, and stand. Make sure to keep things positive and upbeat, and reward him when he does what you ask.

If he wanders off or gets distracted, don't worry. This is normal at first. Stand still and wait quietly for him to turn back to you. Don't fall into the trap of nagging him to pay attention or chasing him down to correct him.

Since you're in a relatively small space, he will soon get bored and check in to see what you're doing. When he looks your way, call him back to you for a treat and lots of praise.

4 ▸ QUIT WHILE YOU'RE AHEAD

Keep the session short and fun, no more than two to three minutes total. Try to quit before your dog gets bored.

5 ▸ PUT THE LEASH BACK ON

Praise and give several treats in a row as soon as the leash is back on. You want your dog to look forward to being leashed again, rather than trying to avoid you when he's loose, so it pays to reward this step handsomely.

Spend several sessions working in this first location to make sure that your dog is performing well before moving on. Remember, there's no rush; take things as slow as you need to.

6 ▸ TRY IT OUTSIDE

Now move to an enclosed outdoor location. A fenced backyard works very well for this, if you have one. If not, practice on a local tennis court, an enclosed playground, or some other fenced-in space.

7 ▸ PRACTICE TO BUILD CONFIDENCE

Repeat steps 1–5 in the new location. Practice this until your dog is happy to stay near you, doing whatever you ask, even when the leash is off. Make sure you continue to praise and reward with very tasty treats when he listens. This is a difficult skill for most dogs!

8 ▸ GIVE YOUR DOG SOME REAL OFF-LEASH TIME

At this point, you can begin allowing your dog off-leash in new places as long as things are going well. When he's running free, call him back to you frequently to "check in." Reward him generously when he listens. Eventually, you should be able to let him run in parks, open fields, or hiking trails if this is allowed in your area.

DOG TRAINING TIP

Always make sure to obey local leash laws, and err on the side of safety if you have any doubts about your dog's ability to stay with you. If you're concerned, just keep him on-leash or use a long line to give him some extra freedom while still staying safe.

FIVE STEPS TO
Troubleshooting Your Training

As with everything else in life, you're bound to hit some speed bumps every now and then in the course of training your dog. It can be frustrating when things aren't going according to plan, but don't worry; in most cases, it's easy to get back on track once you figure out the problem.

If your dog isn't listening when you ask him to do something, there are two possible reasons why. Either he doesn't understand what you want, or you haven't made it worth his while to comply. Really, that's it! So when you run into trouble, look a little more closely at what you've actually taught your dog—usually, he just needs a little help.

To solve a training problem:

1 ▸ CHECK FOR UNDERSTANDING

First, see if your dog really understands what you're asking. If he won't sit for you at the park, try asking him to sit in the living room when you get home. Often, our dogs don't know basic commands as well as we think they do. If he seems confused, just go back to basics and reteach the "sit" command. Spend a few training sessions at home refreshing his memory before trying it again in real life.

Remember that learning is not always a linear process. You may experience occasional "hiccups" where your pup seems to have forgotten everything you've been working on, especially with newer skills. Just go back into training mode and review what you've taught him.

2 ▸ REVIEW DISTRACTION AND GENERALIZATION TRAINING

If the behavior is solid at home but falls apart in other places, it's likely that your dog simply needs more practice to understand what you want. Over time, he can learn to remember his training no matter where he is or what's happening around him—it just takes a bit of extra work on your part.

3 ▸ TRY A DIFFERENT REWARD

If you're having trouble keeping your pup's attention, or if he isn't responding to a cue that he knows well, he may simply not be motivated by what you're offering. Try switching to a higher-value treat or adding in other types of rewards such as toy play or chase games.

4 ▸ GET A CHECKUP WITH YOUR VET

It's always important to rule out physical problems, especially if your pup suddenly becomes less cooperative about something that he previously enjoyed.

Dogs with arthritis or back pain may be physically uncomfortable with sitting or lying down, or they may refuse to stand still for brushing and grooming of sensitive areas. If he doesn't want to jump or fetch, he may have a pulled muscle or a broken tooth. If you can't find an obvious behavioral explanation, give your dog the benefit of the doubt and take him to the vet for a thorough checkup.

5 ▸ ASK A PROFESSIONAL FOR HELP

If you've tried extra practice, better rewards, and your vet says your pup is healthy and fit, then consider doing a few sessions with a good reward-based trainer who can work with you in person. Sometimes, an extra pair of eyes can be invaluable in spotting the problem.

PART III
COOPERATIVE K9s
TRAINING FOR HANDLING AND BASIC CARE

If you're like most dog owners, you probably don't think much about basic pet care tasks like bathing, brushing, or nail trimming, until the time comes to do them and your pup doesn't want to cooperate. Many dogs are nervous, fearful, or even aggressive about simple handling and grooming because they've never been taught what you want them to do.

It might surprise you to know that your dog can easily be trained to cooperate with you when you need to do these things, just like learning to sit or lie down on command. You'll find this easiest if you have a young puppy who's new to the entire process, but even adult dogs with a history of being anxious about handling can learn to relax. This makes things much less stressful for both of you, and much safer as well.

In this section, you'll find easy step-by-step guidelines for teaching your dog to allow every kind of basic care or grooming task that you're likely to encounter—everything from routine dental care to bathing and brushing, nail trimming, and even taking medication. The specific steps are different depending on the task you're working on (teeth brushing, giving a bath, and so forth), but the basic approach is the same in every case: go slowly, be patient, and stay positive.

With a little practice, you (or your vet or groomer) should be able to provide any care your dog needs to keep him clean and healthy!

Standing Still for a Physical Exam

Teaching your dog to stand still for an exam might not seem very flashy or exciting, but you'd be surprised how much easier it makes things at the vet's office. For many dogs, having their body handled can be uncomfortable or scary if they haven't been taught what to expect, which can make it hard for them to get a thorough checkup.

You can also use this skill at home to check your dog regularly for lumps or bumps, skin problems, or other issues that you might not notice otherwise.

To train your dog to stand still for a physical exam:

1 ▸ START WITH YOUR DOG STANDING

If he doesn't know how to stand on cue, see Five Steps to Training "Stand" in Part II for instructions on teaching this skill.

Standing is the best position for an exam, because it allows you (or your veterinarian) to carefully palpate your dog's belly and chest, check the rear legs and tail, and even examine your pup's "private areas" if needed. These things are very hard to do if your dog is sitting on his rear end or wiggling around. Problems can easily be missed without a nice solid stand.

2 ▸ TRY A LIGHT TOUCH

Touch your dog gently on the back with one hand. Praise and reward if he stands still while you do this. If not, just remind him to stand and try again.

3 ▸ STROKE HIS BACK AND SIDES

Repeat step 2 several times, until your dog is confidently holding his position each time you touch his back. Run your hand gently down his back and sides as if you were petting him, with praise and treats for standing still.

4 ▸ WORK UP TO DOING MORE

Try touching his front and rear legs, chest, and belly. Continue to praise and reward after running your hand over each new area.

5 ▸ HANDLE SENSITIVE AREAS GENTLY

Finally, move on to more sensitive parts of his body such as the paws, tail, ears, and genital areas. If he gets nervous and pulls away, just go back to something easier for the next few repetitions and work your way up again. Remember, this can be challenging for many dogs, so go slowly and be patient.

6 ▸ COMPLETE A FULL EXAM

Eventually, you can work your way up to doing a full examination while your dog stands calmly for a single treat at the end. Practice at home at least once a month to make sure your pup remembers what to do. Your veterinarian will thank you for this, and you'll have the satisfaction of knowing that he's getting a thorough checkup at each visit.

Nail Trimming

From our perspective, it can be hard to understand why nail trimming is such a difficult thing for many dogs. After all, if done properly, there's no pain and very little drama. But from your pup's point of view, having his feet handled may be scary and uncomfortable.

DOG TRAINING TIP

Apart from their shape, your dog's nails aren't too different from your own toenails and fingernails. They consist of an outer shell made of hard keratin, surrounding a sensitive "quick" containing the nerve and blood supply. To trim the nail properly, you want to take off just the very tip of the hard keratin sheath. If you cut the nail too short (known as "quicking" the nail), it will hurt your dog and cause the nail to bleed.

If your dog has white toenails, the quick will be visible as a pink area closer to the toe. Make sure to stay in front of the pink part of the nail when you cut. In dogs with black nails, your job is a bit more challenging. Try looking for the part of the nail that tapers into a narrow curve at the end, and trim just this part. If you're unsure how far back to cut, ask your veterinarian or groomer to show you.

If you accidentally quick your dog, don't worry! It happens to everyone occasionally. You can dab a bit of flour or cornstarch or a commercial styptic powder such as Kwik-Stop to stop the bleeding. Give your dog an extra treat for being brave.

Paws are a sensitive part of the body for many dogs, and your dog may not understand why you're trying to touch them. On top of that, if your dog has had bad experiences with nail trims, he will likely remember this and may be frightened of having his toenails cut.

Fortunately, any dog can learn to relax and be comfortable while you gently trim his nails. It just takes some patience and a good training plan.

To teach your dog to stand calmly for nail trims:

1 ▸ GET EVERYTHING READY

For large dogs, you may find it easiest to sit on the floor with him. If your dog is smaller, you could opt to use a grooming table instead. Make sure you have a supply of tasty treats handy, as well as your nail clippers.

If your dog seems nervous as soon as he sees the nail trimmers, spend the first several training sessions allowing your dog to sniff the clippers without doing anything else. Make this a positive experience with lots of praise and treats, and don't move on to the next step until he seems relaxed and comfortable.

2 ▸ TRY TOUCHING THE PAWS

Start by touching one of your dog's paws gently your fingertips, then praise and reward. Do this with each paw separately to make sure that he's comfortable with all four feet being touched before moving on.

If he resists or tries to pull away, don't scold him; this will only make him more anxious. Instead, simply back up a step or two and take it easy. Reward when he is calm again.

3 ▸ INTRODUCE THE CLIPPERS

Gently lift one paw and touch it lightly with the nail clippers. Praise and reward your dog for standing still. Repeat this with each paw in turn. Work your way up to touching each toenail gently, one at a time.

4 ▸ CLIP THE TIP OF ONE TOENAIL

Be very careful not to cut the nail too short, because you might cut into the quick. Cut the tip of the one toenail, then praise and reward once this is done.

It's best not to try and trim all of his nails in the same session, at first. Instead, do one or two nails and then stop. You want to end the session on a high note.

5 ▸ DO A FULL NAIL TRIM

Work up to this step slowly so that you can make sure your dog is comfortable with the process. The first several times you try a complete nail trim, reward with a treat after clipping each nail. All the while make sure your pup is relaxed and happy.

DOG TRAINING TIP

The number of sessions required to complete all five steps of nail trimming will vary from dog to dog. Puppies who are "starting fresh" with no previous history of scary nail trims will likely progress very quickly, while older dogs who have had negative experiences in the past may take considerably longer.

Take as long as your dog needs, and don't rush the process. Being able to do easy, stress-free nail trims for the rest of his life is well worth it.

SIX STEPS TO
Ear Cleaning

Cleaning your dog's ears regularly is an important part of keeping him healthy, especially if he has heavy "drop ears" like a Labrador retriever or cocker spaniel. Done correctly, this should not be a painful procedure for your dog, but it can feel strange to him and may be scary if he isn't accustomed to it. To clean your pup's ears, you can use an over-the-counter ear flush labeled for dogs or you can ask your veterinarian for a recommendation.

To teach your dog to stand quietly for ear cleaning:

1 ▸ GET YOUR SUPPLIES READY

Start by gathering everything you need: ear cleaner, cotton balls or a soft washcloth, and lots of treats.

2 ▸ LET YOUR DOG GET COMFORTABLE

Sit on the floor with your pup, or set up on a couch or chair if you prefer. Allow him to sniff everything if he's curious.

If your dog already has a history of being nervous about ear cleaning, you may need to spend several sessions on this particular step. Praise and reward him for staying near you and looking at everything, and don't go any further until he's calm and relaxed.

3 ▸ TOUCH THE EARS

Gently touch one ear, then praise and reward. Repeat with the other ear. Do this several times until your dog is completely comfortable with this step.

4 ▸ INTRODUCE THE BOTTLE

Pick up the bottle of ear cleaner (still securely closed), and bring it up to your dog's ear as if to squirt some into the ear canal. You don't want to actually use the cleaner yet, so don't open the nozzle. Touch the bottle of cleaner to your dog's ear, then praise and reward.

Your dog may be nervous about this step at first, especially if he has not enjoyed having his ears cleaned in the past. That's okay. Just take your time and go slowly. Repeat this as many times as needed, giving a treat each time, until he's calm and relaxed.

5 ▸ ADD THE CLEANER

Open the bottle of ear cleaner. Gently squirt the recommended number of drops into your dog's ear canal. Praise enthusiastically and reward. This is a strange sensation for most dogs, so your pup may appear startled. Tell him what a good boy he is, and give him lots of treats if he seems nervous.

DOG TRAINING TIP

If your dog's ear appears red and swollen, or if there is a large amount of discharge or a foul odor coming from the ear, these are signs of an ear infection. In that case, see your veterinarian before attempting to clean the ears at home.

An infected ear will be very sore and painful, so don't try to work through the cleaning steps until the infection is resolved.

6 ▸ CLEAN THE EARS

Work up to being able to clean ears. Fill the ear canal with cleaning solution, massage the ear, and then use your cotton balls or wash cloth to wipe away any gunk or discharge. Remove your hands and let your dog shake his head. This is the final step, so give your pup lots of praise and a great reward when you get there! Then repeat the process with the other ear.

Dental Care

Believe me, I know—the idea of brushing your dog's teeth can seem daunting at first, especially if you've never done it. But the truth is, good dental care is just as important for your pup's overall health as it is for yours.

Tartar buildup can lead to painful dental problems such as gingivitis, tooth root infections, and tooth loss. It can even damage internal organs like the heart and kidneys by seeding your dog's bloodstream with bacteria. So starting a good dental care plan early on is well worth it.

To teach your dog to be comfortable having his teeth brushed:

1 ▸ GET YOUR SUPPLIES

Start by selecting a comfortable tooth brush and an appropriate dog-friendly toothpaste. These can be purchased at most pet stores or ordered online. Your veterinarian's office may carry them for sale too. Canine tooth brushes should be very soft so that they don't cause any pain or irritation to the gums.

Make sure to use a toothpaste that is specifically designed for dogs. Human toothpaste has too much fluoride for them and is not safe to use. Most dog toothpastes come in canine-friendly flavors like chicken or beef, so you shouldn't have any trouble finding one that your dog likes.

2 ▸ FIND A COMFORTABLE SPOT TO WORK

Depending on what's easiest for you, you can sit on the floor or put your dog on a grooming table. If he's a small breed, you could even hold him in your lap if you prefer.

3 ▸ LET YOUR DOG TRY THE TOOTHPASTE

Put a small amount of toothpaste on your finger and allow your dog to lick it off. He'll probably think this is a wonderful treat. Repeat this a few times, until your dog is happily wagging his tail at the sight of the toothpaste tube.

4 ▸ RUB YOUR FINGER ACROSS HIS TEETH

Most dogs enjoy this step, as long as they like the toothpaste you're using. Praise your dog and tell him what a good boy he is while you gently touch all of his teeth, from the tiny incisors in the front to the larger molars in the back.

If your dog is comfortable and relaxed, you can gently open his mouth to reach the inside surfaces of the teeth as well. This makes some dogs a bit more nervous, so work up to this gradually.

5 ▸ INTRODUCE THE TOOTHBRUSH

Put a small amount of toothpaste on the brush for your dog to lick off.

DOG TRAINING TIP

If your dog has severe dental disease already (red or swollen gums, exposed tooth roots, pus, or a foul odor coming from his mouth), please see your veterinarian prior to starting a tooth brushing regimen at home.

Brushing your pup's teeth is great for preventing problems down the line and keeping his mouth healthy, but it won't fix existing dental issues. Your veterinarian can perform a complete dental cleaning under anesthesia and will remove any painful or infected teeth so you'll have a clean slate to start with.

6 ▸ GENTLY USE THE BRUSH TO TOUCH HIS TEETH

Repeat step 4, using the toothbrush instead of your finger. This will be a different sensation for your dog, so he might be nervous at first. If he pulls away or seems uncomfortable, stop and go more slowly. You may need to do just one or two teeth at a time, until he gets more accustomed to the brush.

7 ▸ BRUSH THE TEETH REGULARLY TO KEEP THEM CLEAN

Eventually, you can work up to being able to brush all of your dog's teeth easily in one sitting. For best results, make this part of his daily routine, just before bedtime or first thing in the morning as soon as you get up.

FIVE STEPS TO
Bathing Your Dog

Whether your dog is large or small, long-haired or short-haired, or anything in between, there will be times when you need to give him a bath. For many dogs and owners, bathing can be a stressful experience that provokes anxiety on both sides. Most dogs don't enjoy getting wet or being restrained in a scary tub with water running, and no owner enjoys wrestling with a frantic pup who's covered in shampoo and desperate to escape the bathroom.

Fortunately, it doesn't need to be this way. Even if your dog isn't a fan of soap and water, there's no reason he can't learn to relax happily in the bathtub when he needs a good wash.

To teach your dog to stand calmly for a bath:

1 ▸ GET YOUR DOG COMFORTABLE IN THE BATHROOM

Start by bringing your dog into the bathroom and closing the door. If your pup has a history of scary bath experiences, he may become very anxious at this point, and that's okay. Spend several short training sessions sitting with him in the bathroom, praising him and feeding him treats. Don't progress any further until he's happy and relaxed, even with the door closed.

2 ▸ REWARD FOR GETTING IN THE TUB

Take some peanut butter or spray cheese and smear a generous amount on the inside of the bathtub. If your dog is fairly small, pick him up and put him in the tub; if he's larger, show him the yummy treat that's waiting and encourage him to hop in. Allow him to stand in the tub and lick the goodies for a few minutes, then lift him out again.

Remember—no water in the tub just yet. Right now, you should be focusing on getting your dog happy and comfortable in the bathtub. Don't add water until he's happily jumping into the tub on his own, or wagging his tail eagerly for you to lift him in.

3 ▸ INTRODUCE THE WATER

When your dog is happy to hop in the tub and stand there while licking his treat, slowly turn on the water. Make sure it's not too hot or too cold, and keep the stream slow so that he isn't startled by the noise. Tell him what a good boy he is! Run 2 or 3 inches of water into the tub, then stop. Make sure your pup is still happily licking his peanut butter with no signs of stress—if not, repeat this step as often as needed until he's no longer fazed by the water.

4 ▸ WET THE COAT, SHAMPOO, AND RINSE

If your dog is comfortable and relaxed standing in a few inches of water, go ahead and give him a bath. You can pour water over him using a pitcher, or you can wet him down using a handheld sprayer attachment if you have one. Add shampoo, lather, and rinse thoroughly. Just go slowly, and make sure to replenish his supply of peanut butter as often as needed to keep him busy.

5 ▸ FADE OUT THE TREATS

Over time, you can begin to decrease the amount of peanut butter you use for each bath. If your dog seems comfortable, you can eventually phase it out altogether. Just make sure to praise him for standing still in the tub, and watch him closely for any signs of stress. Many dogs learn to enjoy their "spa time" after a while, as long as you're patient and gentle.

EIGHT STEPS TO
Brushing Your Dog

If you have a dog with a short, smooth hair coat like a miniature pinscher or Weimaraner—lucky you! You're free to skip this section.

For the rest of us, though, brushing our dogs is a daily reality of life. This can be a real challenge if your pup gets nervous or won't stand still when the brush comes out. And, unfortunately, basic grooming isn't optional if you want to avoid mats and maintain healthy skin and hair.

Good grooming habits are easy to start with a new puppy, but even adult dogs who may not care much for brushing can learn to relax and stand quietly so that you can groom without a fuss.

To teach your dog to stand still for brushing:

1 ▶ FIND A COMFORTABLE SPOT TO WORK

If your pup is small to medium-sized, you'll probably find it best to use a grooming table—it's much easier on your back than leaning over your dog to reach everything. For large or giant breeds, working on the floor is usually the simplest option.

2 ▶ GATHER YOUR GROOMING TOOLS

At minimum, you'll need a good quality pin brush or wire slicker brush, as well as a spray bottle of water or leave-in conditioner. You may also need a wide-toothed comb, soft bristle brush, or an undercoat rake depending on your dog's coat type.

3 ▸ GET YOUR DOG COMFORTABLE

Put him on the grooming table or bring him to the area where you plan to work. Let him see and sniff the brushes and other grooming tools if he wants. Many dogs are curious about these objects at first. Make sure he's calm and relaxed before moving on to the next step.

4 ▸ ASK YOUR DOG TO STAND

If he doesn't know this cue yet, see Five Steps to Training "Stand" in Part II for instructions on how to teach it.

5 ▸ INTRODUCE THE BRUSH

Lightly stroke your dog's back once with the brush. If he stands still, praise and reward with a treat. If he wiggles or pulls away, ask him to stand and try again. Repeat this step until he can stand solidly without moving at all while you lightly brush his back.

6 ▸ SPRAY LIGHTLY WITH WATER

When he's comfortable being touched by the brush, add in a spritz of water or conditioner; this keeps the fur damp while you're brushing, which is important so as to avoid damaging the coat. Praise and reward him for standing still. Then repeat a single brushstroke down his back, as in step 5.

7 ▸ WORK UP TO THE REST OF HIS BODY

You can gradually progress to brushing his legs, sides, chest, and tail as long as he's doing well. Praise and reward for each few brushstrokes at first, then work up to brushing for longer and longer periods without a treat. If he moves, just remind him to stand and wait until he's comfortable before continuing.

Alternatively, while you brush, you can have a helper stand nearby and feed treats periodically, or hold a spoonful of peanut butter or spray cheese for your dog to lick.

8 ▸ GIVE YOUR DOG A COMPLETE BRUSHING

Eventually, your dog should be able to stand still for an entire brushing session (up to twenty to thirty minutes) for a single treat at the end. Just go slowly and don't rush the process. This is an important life skill for your dog to learn, so it pays to take the time to teach it correctly!

Administering Medication

Even if your dog is healthy at the moment, chances are good that he'll need to take medication at some point in his life: antibiotics for an infection, nonsteroidal anti-inflammatory drugs (NSAIDs) for arthritis, and so forth. Convincing him to swallow a pill can be challenging if you've never had to deal with this before.

Fortunately, medicating your dog doesn't need to be a struggle. With a little planning and foresight, there are lots of things you can do to make this much easier for both of you.

To teach your dog to take medication easily:

1 ▸ COMBINE IT WITH FOOD

Try mixing the meds into a tasty treat, if possible. Liquid medications can usually be mixed with a spoonful of something stinky and delicious, such as canned cat food or liverwurst—this is a very effective way of disguising the taste and convincing your dog to take his medicine voluntarily. Tablets can often be crushed and mixed into soft food like this as well.

Always check with your veterinarian to make sure this is okay, especially when a new medicine is prescribed for your pup. In most cases, it's fine to mix your dog's medication with food. However, there may be some situations when the drug needs to be given on an empty stomach. Other restrictions might limit what you can mix it with. When in doubt, ask.

2 ▸ HIDE IT IN A TREAT

For pills or capsules that can't be crushed, put them inside a soft, smelly treat: a piece of cheese, a slice of hot dog, or commercial Pill Pockets are all good options. If your dog takes the treat gingerly and spits out the medication, try giving several treats in a row. Hide the "medicated" treat in with the others and give them quickly, one after the other, so that he doesn't have time to think too much about chewing.

3 ▸ TRAIN YOUR DOG TO TAKE THE MEDS

If your dog won't take medication hidden in food, you can teach him to allow you to administer the meds on their own. This doesn't need to be stressful or unpleasant; just teach him what to expect, and make sure to reward him afterward for cooperating.

For pills, start by "pilling" your dog with treats to help him get used to the procedure. Open his mouth, place a piece of cheese or meat on the back of his tongue, and use your finger to gently push it down. If you're nervous about your technique, ask your vet to show you how. Once your dog is comfortable with letting you give him a treat "pill," use the same procedure for the real thing. Praise and reward with a yummy treat after he's done.

For liquid medications, ask your veterinarian for an oral syringe with which you can practice. Draw up a small amount of something tasty, such as chicken or beef broth, and use the syringe to give it to your dog. Gently place the tip of the syringe in the back corner of his mouth, then depress the plunger to squirt in the liquid. Go slowly so that he has time to swallow without getting choked. Once he's comfortable with this, use the same technique to give liquid medication when you need to. Again, praise and reward with a treat immediately afterward.

EIGHT STEPS TO
Muzzle Training

If your dog has aggression issues or, for instance, becomes stressed or anxious at the vet's office, wearing a muzzle comfortably can be a very valuable ability for him to have. If you're nervous, don't be—this is usually an easy thing to teach.

In order to practice at home, you will need to purchase a muzzle that fits your dog snugly without being too tight. Most pet stores carry a selection of muzzles in different sizes and styles, or you can order one online. For most situations, a basket-style muzzle that allows a dog to pant, drink water, and eat treats easily is best.

To teach your dog to comfortably wear a muzzle:

1 ▸ INTRODUCE THE MUZZLE

Start by holding the muzzle in your hand. Show it to your dog and allow him to sniff it.

If your pup has had any negative experiences in the past with muzzles, you may need to spend several sessions doing this before going any further. Praise and reward him for looking at the muzzle or touching it with his nose. Don't move on until he is happily approaching for treats and praise whenever you get it out.

2 ▸ SHAPE THE BEHAVIOR YOU WANT

Show your dog the muzzle while holding a treat through the front end. Your dog should readily put his nose into the muzzle to eat the treat. Praise and reward him when he does this.

3 ▸ PRACTICE TO BUILD CONFIDENCE

Repeat step 2 several times, until your dog is happily pushing his entire nose into the muzzle as soon as you hold it out.

4 ▸ START BUILDING DURATION

Begin asking your dog to keep his nose in the muzzle for a few seconds at a time. Get a handful of treats and quickly feed them to your pup one at a time through the end of the muzzle while he keeps his nose in place.

If he gets nervous and pulls away, that's okay. Don't scold him or try to force the issue. Just back up a few steps, take it easy, and work your way back up.

5 ▸ BUCKLE THE STRAPS

When he's comfortable holding his nose in the muzzle for several seconds, try buckling the straps behind his ears. Praise and reward him with a handful of treats in quick succession, then immediately remove the muzzle.

6 ▸ PRACTICE TAKING THE MUZZLE ON AND OFF

Repeat step 5 several times, until your dog seems comfortable with having the muzzle buckled on and removed. Make sure to feed several treats each time while the muzzle is on, which helps build a positive association with wearing it.

7 ▸ LEAVE THE MUZZLE ON

Try leaving the muzzle on and buckled for short periods, no more than a few minutes at first. Keep your dog distracted with something else to help keep him from pawing at the muzzle or being bothered by it. Take him for a quick walk, or ask him for several easy obedience behaviors in a row.

8 ▶ USE THE MUZZLE IN REAL LIFE

Eventually, your dog should be comfortable wearing his muzzle for up to thirty minutes or more at a time. You can use it for vet visits, grooming appointments, or training sessions as needed, depending on your pup's specific issues.

PART IV
JUST FOR FUN
TRICKS AND GAMES

Now that your dog has learned some basic obedience and handling skills, let's move on to some fun and games. Teaching your dog a few simple tricks and games is a great way to keep busy on a rainy day, exercise your pup's brain, and strengthen your bond. These skills are also perfect for showing off to your friends and family—an added bonus!

In the following pages, you'll find easy, step-by-step instructions for training your dog to do a variety of different tricks, from simple beginner skills like "shake" and "speak," to more challenging behaviors like balancing a treat on his nose or commando-crawling on the floor. Remember, these tricks can be taught to both young and old dogs. Regardless of your pup's current skill set, energy level, or body type, you should be able to find several tricks that are a good fit for both of you to try.

You can enjoy teaching the skills described in this section for their own sake, or you can use them as a jumping off point for more advanced training for dog sports like agility, rally obedience, or canine freestyle. As long as you and your pup are both having fun, how far you go is up to you!

Training "Shake"

Learning how to "shake," or give a paw when asked, is a fun and easy behavior for most dogs. If you've never taught your pup any tricks before, this is a great one to start with. It's usually quick and simple to teach.

Once this skill is learned, your dog can show it off whenever he meets someone new. Kids, in particular, love it when a dog will shake for them!

To teach your dog to shake on cue:

1 ▸ START WITH YOUR DOG IN A SIT

You can stand or kneel in front of him, depending on his size and what's most comfortable for you.

2 ▸ ENTICE HIM WITH A TREAT

Hold a tasty treat in your closed fist, just in front of your dog's nose. Make sure that the treat is something smelly and enticing—you want your dog to be excited about getting it.

3 ▸ LET HIM SNIFF YOUR HAND

Don't say anything or give any other prompting at this stage. Just keep your hand still and wait.

4 ▸ WAIT FOR YOUR DOG TO LIFT HIS PAW

After a few seconds, most dogs will try pawing at your hand in an effort to get the food. Immediately praise your pup as soon as he does this, and open your hand to let him have the treat.

5 ▸ PRACTICE TO BUILD CONFIDENCE

Repeat this sequence several times, until your dog is confidently pawing at your closed fist as soon as you present it.

6 ▸ ADD THE VERBAL CUE

Say, "Shake" as you hold out your fist, and praise and reward when your dog paws at it.

7 ▸ FADE OUT THE FOOD

Say, "Shake" and try presenting your closed fist as usual, but without a treat inside this time.

8 ▸ REWARD WHEN HE GETS IT RIGHT

When your dog paws at your fist, praise him and reward with a treat from your other hand.

9 ▸ MAKE SURE HE UNDERSTANDS THE GAME

Repeat this sequence several times. Your dog should know at this point that there is no treat in your fist but will paw it to earn a reward from your other hand. This is exactly what you want.

10 ▸ TRY IT WITH AN OPEN HAND

Now say, "Shake" and try presenting your open hand, palm up, rather than closed in a fist. Your dog may seem a bit uncertain at first, but he should still put his paw on your hand. Praise enthusiastically and reward with a treat.

11 ▸ PRACTICE WITH NEW PEOPLE

Once he knows how to shake for you, you can ask friends or visitors to try it too. Most dogs enjoy showing off their skills, especially if there are treats involved.

Training "Roll Over"

Having your dog roll over on cue is a classic, showy parlor trick that impresses even non-dog lovers. The mechanics of this trick aren't really difficult, but some dogs can be worried or anxious at first about flipping over onto their back, so be patient and don't be afraid to go slowly.

To teach your dog to roll over:

1 ▸ START WITH YOUR DOG IN A DOWN POSITION

If he doesn't know this skill yet, see Eight Steps to Training "Down" in Part II for instructions on how to teach your dog to lie down on cue.

Use a mat or carpeted area when first teaching this behavior, if possible. This will be much more comfortable on your dog's back, and it will give him better traction for propelling his body over.

2 ▸ SHAPE A HEAD TURN

Using a treat in your hand, slowly lure his nose to one side and back toward his shoulder. As his nose follows the lure, he should flop over onto one hip. Praise and reward him as soon as this happens.

3 ▸ LURE YOUR DOG ONTO HIS SIDE

Repeat step 2 several times, gradually moving the treat farther and farther back toward his shoulder until he lies all the way over on his side.

For most dogs, you will need to shape this gradually in several steps. Make sure to reward each repetition with a treat, and progress as slowly as your dog needs. If he gets confused and stands up, just start again from a down position and make things a bit easier next time.

4 ▸ FOLLOW THE TREAT ALL THE WAY OVER

Repeat step 3, and continue to move the treat in your hand in a complete circle over his back—as his nose follows the treat, he should roll all the way over. This is the hardest part, so be patient.

If your dog is nervous about this step, allow him to nibble the treat continuously and move your hand very, very slowly. It may take several tries before he rolls all the way over.

5 ▸ PRACTICE TO BUILD CONFIDENCE

Repeat step 4 several times, until your dog is confidently rolling all the way over to follow your hand.

6 ▸ INTRODUCE THE COMMAND

At this point, you can add the verbal cue, "Roll over" just before luring him through the exercise.

7 ▸ FADE OUT THE TREAT

When things are going well, try using your empty hand (no treat) to guide your dog to roll over. Praise and reward when he does.

8 ▸ SHOW OFF HIS NEW SKILL

Eventually, with practice, he should learn to roll over happily with just the verbal cue and your hand signal. Enjoy showing off this flashy trick to your friends!

Training "Crawl"

Teaching your dog to belly-crawl along the floor is a fun trick that's easy to train. Once this behavior is learned, you can use it to ask your dog to crawl under things. You can also use it in combination with other tricks like roll over or play dead. It's great for teaching body awareness too, since your pup has to think about what all of his legs are doing and keep his belly against the floor to do it correctly.

To teach your dog to crawl:

1 ▸ START WITH YOUR DOG IN A DOWN POSITION

If he doesn't know how to lie down on command, see Eight Steps to Training "Down" in Part II for instructions on how to teach this behavior before moving on.

2 ▸ LURE HIS NOSE DOWN TO THE FLOOR

Hold a treat in front of your dog's nose, and lower it to the floor between his front paws. This should encourage him to look down and keep his chin near the floor.

3 ▸ MOVE THE TREAT SLOWLY

Slowly pull the treat forward along the ground, just an inch or two at first. It's important not to move too quickly or your dog will stand up to go after the treat. You want him to stay in a down position, so keep your treat low and let him nibble it as you move your hand.

4 ▶ REWARD FOR STRETCHING OUT

As your dog flattens out and stretches forward with his nose, praise him and let him have the treat. Repeat this step several times, until he's confidently lowering his head and stretching forward.

5 ▶ REWARD FOR WRIGGLING FORWARD

Now try moving the treat just a little farther. Your dog should wriggle forward a bit to follow it. This is exactly what you want. Praise and reward at the first sign of any movement.

6 ▶ ASK FOR MORE MOVEMENT

Repeat step 5 several times in a row, moving the treat just a bit farther each time. Your dog should get progressively more confident about shimmying forward on his belly to get the reward.

If he gets confused and stands up, don't worry. This is a normal part of the learning process. Just remove the treat, ask him to lie down again, and start over. Make things a bit easier for the next few repetitions to help him be successful.

As you increase the distance he needs to crawl, it may take him some time to figure out how to move his body toward the treat without standing up. Be patient!

7 ▶ INTRODUCE THE COMMAND

Give the verbal cue, "Crawl" just before moving the treat. Over time, with lots of practice, he will learn to associate this word with the act of crawling on his belly.

8 ▶ ADD SOME CHALLENGES

Work up to asking your dog to crawl for several feet before getting his reward. To make things more interesting, you can also add in simple obstacles for him to crawl under, like a chair or low platform. Be creative and have fun. Your dog will enjoy the added challenges.

Training "Sit Pretty"

Sitting pretty, or the "sit up and beg" position, is another fun trick to spend some time on if you're stuck indoors with a bored dog. If he knows how to sit, you're ready to get started.

To teach your dog to sit pretty:

1 ▸ START WITH YOUR DOG IN A SIT

If he doesn't know how to sit on cue yet, teach him this first. (See Seven Steps to Training "Sit" in Part II for detailed instructions.)

2 ▸ LURE THE NOSE UP

Hold a treat in front of your dog's nose, and slowly move it back and upward over his head. He should look up and shift his weight back a bit in order to follow the treat. Praise and reward.

DOG TRAINING TIP

Some breeds, especially long-backed dogs like corgis, dachshunds, and basset hounds, may not be able to do the "sit pretty" trick safely due to the strain it can place on their spine. If your dog has a history of back issues such as a "slipped" or herniated disc or spinal arthritis, it's probably best to skip this training. If you have any concerns, check with your vet before going ahead.

3 ▸ SLOWLY RAISE THE TREAT

Once he's doing this easily, try raising the treat an inch or two above his head. Go slowly and let him nibble the treat the entire time if needed. This keeps his nose right against your fingers, which is important.

4 ▸ REWARD FOR ONE FRONT PAW OFF THE GROUND

As your raise the treat, your dog should begin leaning back and stretching his nose upward to follow it. Watch for one front paw to come slightly off the ground. Praise and reward immediately as soon as this happens.

5 ▸ REWARD FOR BOTH FRONT PAWS OFF THE GROUND

Repeat step 4 several times, gradually moving the treat a bit higher with each repetition. After a few tries, your dog should be able to get both front paws slightly off the ground. Praise and reward for this.

6 ▸ SHAPE THE "SIT PRETTY" POSITION

Continue to gradually move the food lure higher over the next several tries. Your pup will stretch up a bit farther each time, until eventually he's able to reach the full "sitting up" position: resting his weight on his haunches, with his front paws held up in front of him.

This behavior comes very easily to some dogs, while others need a lot of practice to learn how to keep their balance. Go as slowly as your dog needs, and always take a break if he seems to be getting tired or frustrated.

7 ▸ START BUILDING DURATION

Once your dog can sit up easily, you can work on building duration in this position. Try feeding treats rapid-fire, one after the other, as long as he stays up—this will help him learn to hold the position rather than immediately dropping back down again.

8 ▸ INTRODUCE THE COMMAND

Give the verbal cue, "Sit pretty" just before luring him up into position with the treat. Over time, he will begin to understand and offer this behavior when you give the verbal command alone.

9 ▸ SHOW OFF HIS NEW SKILL

Eventually, you can work up to asking your dog to sit pretty for several seconds at a time before giving a treat. This is an easy trick for kids and visitors to do with your pup, and one that many dogs enjoy. So have fun, and let him show off what he can do.

SIX STEPS TO
Training "Speak"

If your dog likes to bark, this trick will likely come very naturally to him. Some dogs are quite easy to teach to bark on cue (especially vocal breeds like beagles or shelties) while others may find this skill more challenging. Either way, it's something you and your dog can have fun practicing if you want to give it a try.

To teach your dog to speak on cue:

1 ▸ FIGURE OUT WHAT MAKES YOUR DOG BARK

Try getting him excited about a toy, holding a tasty treat just out of reach, or even knocking on the door—whatever works! Once you have a consistent way to prompt your dog to start barking, you're ready to begin.

2 ▸ TRIGGER THE BARK, THEN REWARD

Get your dog excited, then praise and reward with a treat as soon as he barks. It may take him a few repetitions to figure out what's being rewarded. Many dogs don't really seem to be consciously aware that they're barking, at first.

3 ▸ PRACTICE TO BUILD HIS CONFIDENCE

Repeat this sequence several times. You should notice that as he starts to catch on it will take less and less prompting to get your dog to bark.

4 ▶ INTRODUCE THE COMMAND

When you're sure that you can easily elicit a bark with your chosen prompt, you can introduce the verbal cue, "Speak" just before you get your dog excited. Praise and reward as soon as he barks.

5 ▶ FADE OUT THE EXTRA PROMPT

Try saying, "Speak" and then wait a few seconds without doing anything else. If your dog barks, praise and reward enthusiastically. If he seems puzzled and does not bark within ten to fifteen seconds, go ahead and prompt him again with whatever you were doing before: door knocking, toy waving, or whatever it was. Repeat several more times with the prompt, then try it again with the verbal cue alone.

6 ▶ TAKE IT ON THE ROAD

When your dog is confidently barking every time as soon as you say, "Speak," you can try out your new trick in other places—different parts of the house, out on a walk, etc. Visitors and people you meet outside may also enjoy asking your dog to speak.

DOG TRAINING TIP

When you first teach the "speak" trick, you may notice that your dog barks at you more often in general when he wants a treat. He is "offering" this behavior to see if it works, since you've been rewarding it recently in your training sessions. This is normal and will go away on its own once the novelty of his new trick wears off. Just make sure that you never reward him for barking unless you have asked him to "speak."

FIVE STEPS TO
Training "Back Up"

Teaching your dog to back up can be handy if your dog tends to get underfoot when you're busy around the house or if he's standing in your way and you need him to move. It's also an important foundation behavior if you're interested in doing any dog sports with your pup, like rally obedience or freestyle.

To teach your dog to back up on cue:

1 ▸ START WITH YOUR DOG STANDING IN FRONT OF YOU

If your dog doesn't yet know how to "stand," see Five Steps to Training "Stand" in Part II for instructions on how to teach this position.

2 ▸ STEP TOWARD YOUR DOG

Stand close to your dog, facing him, and take a small step forward into his personal space. Most dogs will respond to this by leaning back or taking a small step backward. Praise and reward with a treat as soon as you see any movement.

Some dogs have a larger personal "space bubble" than others. If he doesn't move backward at first, take another tiny step closer. Repeat until you're almost on top of him, if needed. Eventually he'll move. Just go slowly and make sure not to scare him or step on his paws.

3 ▸ PRACTICE TO BUILD CONFIDENCE

Repeat this exercise until your dog is eagerly backing up as soon as you step forward. Make sure to praise and reward each time to help him understand what you want.

4 ▸ INTRODUCE THE COMMAND

Add the verbal cue, "Back up," along with a hand signal, if you wish. You can use both hands in front of your chest, palms out, in a pushing motion. This is an easy visual signal for your dog to see, and it's also an easy gesture for most owners to remember.

5 ▸ ADD SOME CHALLENGES

When your dog is good at backing up when asked to from a standing position, you can make things a bit harder. Try asking him to "Back up" from a sit or down position—this is much more challenging, since he has to stand up before he can move backward. Make sure to praise and reward, as usual, when he gets it right.

Training to Balance a Treat

This is a fun trick that most people find very impressive. To balance a treat on his nose, your dog needs to have a solid "stay" behavior and a lot of self-control. It's a great way to show off your pup's willpower, since he has to hold his position and resist the treat until you release him.

To teach your dog to balance a treat on his nose:

1 ▸ START WITH YOUR DOG IN A SIT

You can stand or sit in front of your dog, depending on his size and what's most comfortable.

2 ▸ PLACE THE TREAT

Gently hold his muzzle (the long part of his nose) with one hand, and place a treat on top of his nose with the other.

At first, use a fairly low-value treat such as a Milk-Bone for this trick. This will be easier for your dog to resist. As he gets better at controlling himself, you can gradually work up to more difficult challenges like pieces of cheese or hot dog slices.

3 ▸ KEEP YOUR DOG STILL WITH THE "STAY" COMMAND

If he doesn't know this command yet, see Six Steps to Training "Stay" in Part II for instructions on how to teach it. Wait one second, then praise and give him the treat.

If your dog seems nervous about having you touch his muzzle, or if he pulls away when you try to do this, don't scold him. Take a few sessions to work on this skill by itself; gently touch his muzzle, then immediately praise and reward. Work on this until he is comfortable allowing you to handle his muzzle before moving on.

4 ▸ WAIT A BIT LONGER

Repeat step 3, but wait two seconds before releasing and giving the treat. Then three seconds, then four, and so on.

5 ▸ LET GO OF HIS MUZZLE

When your dog is comfortable keeping the treat on his nose for several seconds with your hand gently holding his muzzle, try letting go for just a moment—then immediately praise and give him the treat.

6 ▸ KEEP BUILDING DURATION

Repeat step 5 several times, gradually adding more time before praising and rewarding your dog. At this stage, he should be balancing the treat all by himself without any help from you.

If he fidgets once you remove your hand, causing the treat to fall, just pick it up quickly before he can get it. No need to scold him. Just laugh and try again. Remember, this should be a fun game for both of you.

7 ▸ ADD THE RELEASE CUE

At this point, you can begin releasing him with a cheerful verbal cue. Say, "Okay" to allow him to eat the treat on his own, rather than you taking it from his nose and giving it to him.

8 ▸ GIVE YOUR DOG SOME SPACE

Work your way up to placing the treat on his nose and standing back to let him balance the treat for several seconds before releasing him by saying, "Okay." This is an easy trick to show off at home or on the road, once your pup has it down.

SEVEN STEPS TO

Training Your Dog to "Give a Kiss"

For dogs who are naturally affectionate and enjoy licking when they greet people, learning to "give a kiss" on cue is an easy task. But even if your pup doesn't normally do this on his own, you can still teach him to offer a doggy kiss in exchange for a treat.

To train your dog to give kisses:

1 ▸ GET YOUR TREATS READY

Start by finding some type of sticky treat that your dog enjoys. Some possible options would include peanut butter, spray cheese, or cream cheese. For our purposes here, we'll assume you're using peanut butter, but feel free to choose whatever your dog likes best.

2 ▸ GIVE YOUR DOG A TASTE

Dip your finger lightly in the peanut butter, and allow your dog to lick it off. Do this a few times to make sure you have his attention and he's expecting a treat.

3 ▸ DAB SOME PEANUT BUTTER ON YOUR NOSE

Let your pup see you do this, so he knows a treat is there.

4 ▸ LET HIM LICK IT OFF

Give your verbal cue. Say, "Give me a kiss" and lean down so your dog can lick your nose—he should do this readily. Praise and reward with another treat from your hand (such as a piece of chicken or hot dog) as soon as he licks you.

This second treat is important, because you'll be phasing out the peanut butter lure as soon as your dog catches on. Don't skip it.

5 ▸ PRACTICE TO BUILD CONFIDENCE

Repeat step 4 several times, until he's eagerly licking your nose as soon as you give the verbal cue. Make sure you continue to praise and reward with a separate treat each time he gets it right.

6 ▸ FADE OUT THE LURE

Now try it without the peanut butter. Say, "Give me a kiss" and lean down toward your dog, just like before. He should lick your nose, even though there's no treat in sight. Praise and reward immediately when he does.

If he seems confused, don't worry—this can be a tough leap at first for some dogs. Just go back to dabbing peanut butter on your nose for the next few repetitions, then try again.

7 ▸ USE IT FOR REAL-LIFE GREETINGS

With practice, your pup should be able to happily give kisses to anyone who asks. Many dogs and visitors alike enjoy this trick, so feel free to use it as part of your pup's greeting ritual if you wish.

DOG TRAINING TIP

Some dogs may be anxious at first about having you (or someone else) leaning down toward their face—watch your pup's body language for any signs of unease such as crouching down, looking away, tucking the tail, and the like. If he seems nervous about this, you can try crouching down and letting him approach you, rather than you leaning over him. Or skip this "give a kiss" trick altogether, if you prefer!

Training "Jump" (Through a Hoop)

If you have an athletic dog with lots of energy, this trick is a breeze to teach. It's a flashy show-stopper that's also great for tiring out your pup inside when you can't go for a walk. It's also a starting point for more advanced training in dog sports like agility or freestyle.

To train your dog to jump through a hoop:

1 ▸ FIND (OR MAKE) A SUITABLE HOOP

Hula-Hoops come in different sizes and are a popular choice, but you could also make your own hoop using a pool noodle or plastic tubing. Whatever your choice, the hoop should be large enough for your dog to jump through easily without touching.

2 ▸ ENLIST A HELPER

Have your helper hold the hoop in an upright position, with the bottom touching the ground.

3 ▸ LURE YOUR DOG THROUGH THE HOOP

Stand on the opposite side of the hoop from your dog, and use a treat to encourage him to come through. Praise and reward him as soon as he comes to you.

4 ▸ PRACTICE TO BUILD CONFIDENCE

Repeat step 3 several times, until your dog is happily walking through the hoop each time to get the treat.

5 ▸ RAISE THE HOOP A BIT

Have your helper hold the hoop a bit higher—just an inch or two off the ground at first.

6 ▸ HELP YOUR DOG HOP THROUGH

Practice calling your dog through the hoop several more times. At this stage, he may need to hop just a bit to go through the hoop. Praise and reward when he does this.

If he gets confused and goes around, go back to step 3 and try again with the hoop touching the ground. Let him do a few successful repetitions at this level, then try raising the hoop again.

7 ▸ INTRODUCE THE COMMAND

When your dog is confidently hopping back and forth through the hoop, you can add the verbal cue for this behavior. Say, "Jump" as he approaches the hoop, and praise and reward him as soon as he hops through.

8 ▸ ADD MORE HEIGHT

Gradually raise the hoop a bit higher each time, as long as your dog is doing well. Eventually, most dogs should be able to comfortably jump their own height at the shoulder, so if your pup is 16" tall when measured to the top of his shoulder blades, he should be able to jump around 16" safely.

9 ▸ FADE OUT YOUR HELPER

Try holding the hoop yourself instead of having a helper do it. This may be harder for your dog at first, so be patient. Start again with the hoop touching the ground to make things easier, since the overall picture now will look very different to your dog. Say, "Jump" and use your other hand to lure him through with a treat if needed. Praise and reward when he gets it right.

10 ▸ ADD MORE HEIGHT (AGAIN!)

Slowly begin raising the hoop again, making sure to praise and give a treat every time your dog jumps through. Eventually, you can work your way back up to his full jumping height.

11 ▸ TRY SOME NEW CHALLENGES

Once your dog is good at this trick, feel free to be creative. Try having family members hold additional hoops so that he has to jump through several of them in a row, or see if he can run through a hoop that's rolling on the ground. Just remember to keep it positive, and don't be afraid to back up and make things easier if your pup gets confused.

Training Hide and Seek

Teaching your dog to play hide and seek is a fun way to keep him busy when you can't go outside for a walk. He can learn to find you wherever you're hiding. Most dogs really enjoy this game, and it's easy to teach in a few short sessions.

To train your dog to play hide and seek:

1 ▶ ENLIST A HELPER TO HOLD YOUR DOG

Ask a friend or family member to help with this, if you can. If you don't have anyone available, you can also try scattering a handful of treats or kibble on the floor to keep your dog busy for a few minutes while you hide.

2 ▶ MAKE YOUR FIRST "HIDE" EASY

Go somewhere just out of sight: around the corner or in the next room.

3 ▶ CALL YOUR DOG IN A HAPPY VOICE

Your helper should let go as soon as you call, so that your dog can run to find you.

4 ▶ PRAISE AND REWARD FOR SUCCESS

When your pup finds you (even though it's very easy at first!), tell him how smart he is and give him a treat.

5 ▶ PRACTICE TO BUILD CONFIDENCE

Repeat steps 2–4 a few times to make sure that your dog understands the general idea of the game. He should be running enthusiastically to find you as soon as your helper lets him go.

If you prefer, after the first few repetitions you can have your assistant encourage your dog to find you while you stay silent. This is a great way to teach him to "find Mom/Dad." Make sure that you tell him how clever he is and reward with a treat when he finds you.

6 ▶ MAKE THINGS MORE CHALLENGING

This is where the game gets fun! Try hiding someplace fairly simple at first: behind a door or a piece of furniture. Praise and reward your pup each time for finding you.

7 ▶ TRY "HIDING" FOR REAL

Now try hiding in creative places that will really make him think— inside a wardrobe, under a pile of clothes on the bed, or in a closet with the door closed. Many dogs will begin to use their nose to sniff you out at this point, which is always fun to see.

8 ▶ TRY WHOLE-HOUSE SEARCHES

With practice, you can work up to having your dog search the entire house for you. This is a great game for kids to play with your pup. It's also a handy way of tiring him out and making him use his brain.

NINE STEPS TO
Training "Find It"

For most dogs, using their nose to search out treats is a skill that comes naturally. Whether your pup is a born-and-bred scenting dog like a beagle or basset hound or a nontraditional sniffing breed like a pug or Boston terrier, his sense of smell is amazingly acute—hundreds of times more sensitive than even the most discerning human nose.

In a few easy training sessions, you can harness this talent for a game that you and your pup will both enjoy. This game is a great way to keep your dog busy and provide him with some mental stimulation when it's too cold or rainy for a walk. This is also a terrific game to play if your pup is on restricted exercise for a medical issue. Odds are, he'll appreciate the extra snacks as well.

To train your dog to play "find it":

1 ▸ START IN A ROOM BY YOURSELF

A living room or den usually works best for this game, since it gives you lots of options for hiding spots as your dog progresses.

2 ▸ PLACE A TREAT ON THE FLOOR IN PLAIN VIEW

You want this to be very easy for your pup, at first.

3 ▸ BRING IN YOUR DOG

Let your dog into the room and tell him, "Find it." If you need to, show him the treat on the floor; he should grab it happily.

4 ▸ PRACTICE TO BUILD CONFIDENCE

Repeat steps 2–3 several times, until your dog is charging in and finding the treat on the floor without any assistance from you.

5 ▸ VARY THE PLACEMENT OF THE TREAT

Put the treat a few feet away from your previous spot, still in plain view on the floor. Have your dog come in as you verbally cue him by saying, "Find it," as before.

6 ▸ DO A FEW MORE EASY PRACTICE RUNS

Repeat step 5 several times. Make sure that your dog is coming into the room and immediately searching along the floor as soon as you give the verbal cue. He needs to understand the game before you make things any harder.

7 ▸ INCREASE THE CHALLENGE

Try putting the treat in different places—on the coffee table, behind a chair leg, etc. At this point, your dog will need to begin using his nose rather than just doing a quick visual scan. Make sure to praise him and tell him how amazing he is when he finds his prize.

8 ▸ MAKE THE TREAT EVEN HARDER TO FIND

Eventually, you can work your way up to hiding the treat in harder-to-reach places. Wedge it between two couch cushions, under a book on a low shelf, or in a basket of stuffed animals. If your dog gets confused, just back up a few steps and make things easier, then try again.

9 ▸ TRY IT WITH DIFFERENT PEOPLE AND PLACES

Once your dog really catches on, he should be able to find the treat virtually anywhere—so have fun and be creative. Use different rooms in the house, more challenging hiding spots, and have different family members take part in the game.

Training "Which Hand?"

This trick is another fun way for your dog to use his nose. If you have a dog that was bred for scenting, like a bloodhound or harrier, it's likely that he'll really enjoy this game. But even the least scent-oriented dog has a much better nose than any human and can easily learn this game too.

To teach your dog to play "which hand?":

1 ▸ START WITH YOUR DOG IN A SIT

You can stand in front of him, or sit or kneel on the floor if you prefer. Make sure you have a supply of treats handy. Hot dog slices or pieces of lunchmeat work well for this game, since your dog can smell them easily.

2 ▸ ENTICE YOUR PUP WITH A TREAT

Show your dog a treat and let him sniff it, then close your fist around the treat so that he can't get to it.

3 ▸ WAIT FOR HIM TO USE HIS PAW

Allow your pup to sniff and lick at your closed fist. Eventually, most dogs will paw at your hand. As soon as he does this, praise him and open your hand to let him have the treat.

If you've already taught your dog how to "shake," using the instructions earlier in this part, this step should go very quickly.

4 ▸ PRACTICE TO BUILD CONFIDENCE

Repeat step 3 several times, until your dog is pawing at your fist every time you present it. Alternate which hand you're using so that he doesn't become fixated on one hand or the other.

5 ▸ NOW INTRODUCE THE GAME

Make a fist with both hands—one containing a treat, the other empty.

6 ▸ PRESENT YOUR HANDS FOR INSPECTION

Hold both closed fists out in front of your dog. At this stage, he will likely just paw randomly at one of them; this is okay! He doesn't understand the game yet, but he'll figure out with practice.

7 ▸ LET YOUR DOG CHOOSE A HAND

Whichever fist he paws at first, open it. If it contains the treat, praise and let him have it. If not, just say, "Oh, no!" or something similar, and take both hands away. Wait a few seconds, then try again. Don't scold your dog if he doesn't guess correctly. This should be a fun game for both of you, so just laugh and try again if he makes a mistake.

8 ▸ WATCH HIM FIGURE OUT THE RULES

Repeat step 7 several times. It may take several practice sessions, but your dog will eventually realize that he only gets the reward if he correctly chooses which hand it's in. You should start to see him sniffing your hands more closely before pawing the one with the treat; this is what you want.

9 ▸ PLAY "WHICH HAND?" FOR FUN

Eventually, he should become very confident about checking both hands and then making his choice. Many dogs are very good at this game once they understand how it works. Try it with different types of treats, and let friends and family members try it too.

PART V
TROUBLE IN PARADISE
UNDERSTANDING AND ADDRESSING BEHAVIORAL PROBLEMS

In the earlier parts of this book, we focused mainly on the "easy" part of dog training—basic obedience, tricks, and handling issues. We also addressed some normal training problems that are common and expected. This is important information, and I hope you've found it helpful.

But what if you have a dog with a more serious issue? A dog who bites people, attacks other dogs, or destroys your home every time you leave, or a dog who is so terrified of car rides or vet visits that he vomits and urinates on himself. These are real problems, experienced by some dog owners every day, and they can make life very difficult for everyone involved.

If your pup does have severe behavioral problems, you may feel frustrated, embarrassed, and even hopeless at times. This is normal, so don't beat yourself up. Make no mistake, these are challenging issues to deal with. However, in the vast majority of cases they can be managed and treated successfully with a good training plan.

In this final section, we discuss a variety of different behavioral problems, including aggression, anxiety, leash reactivity, and compulsive behavioral issues. Here we give you practical solutions you can implement right away. We'll also address real-life considerations, like finding a qualified behavioral professional in your area and whether medication might be helpful for your dog.

So take heart, and don't give up! No matter what the problem is, there are always things you can do to help.

BEHAVIORAL PROFESSIONALS

My goal in this portion of the book is to give you simple, actionable suggestions for managing your dog's behavioral issues. There's definitely a lot you can do on your own. But it's important to realize that sometimes you need some hands-on guidance from an expert.

FINDING A
Behavioral Professional to Help

If your dog has actually bitten a human or another dog, is injuring himself or causing damage to your home due to anxiety issues, or if you're having trouble making progress with the problem yourself, you should definitely consider finding a qualified trainer or behaviorist who can help you in person.

Behavioral professionals who may be able assist you would include:

1 ▸ VETERINARY BEHAVIORISTS

These are veterinarians who have completed an additional two- to three-year specialized residency program after graduation and have passed a national board exam in the field of veterinary behavior. They are the behavior specialists of the veterinary world and are highly qualified to treat problems such as aggression, anxiety, and compulsive behaviors.

In the United States, veterinary behaviorists can be identified by the initials DACVB after their name, which stands for Diplomate of the American College of Veterinary Behaviorists. You can search for one in your area through the American College of Veterinary Behaviorists (ACVB) website: www.dacvb.org.

If you don't have a board-certified veterinary behaviorist in your area, you can also consider working with a veterinarian who is a member of the American Veterinary Society of Animal Behavior (AVSAB). Although they are not specialists, these veterinarians typically have some additional knowledge and training on behavior. Most likely, they can help you set up a treatment plan and/or prescribe medication for behavioral issues if needed. You can search for an AVSAB member in your area through the website: www.avsab.org.

2 ▸ APPLIED ANIMAL BEHAVIORISTS

These are behavioral professionals who hold doctorate-level degrees (PhDs) in the field of animal behavior. They are extremely knowledgeable about canine behavioral issues and well-qualified to help you put together a detailed treatment plan for your dog's problem.

Applied animal behaviorists in the United States are certified by the Animal Behavior Society, and they will have the initials CAAB after their name, which stands for Certified Applied Animal Behaviorists. You can find a complete directory of applied animal behaviorists in the United States here: www.animalbehaviorsociety.org.

3 ▸ CERTIFIED BEHAVIOR CONSULTANTS

These are professionals who have been certified through an organization such as the International Association of Animal Behavior Consultants (IAABC) or the Certification Council for Professional Dog Trainers (CCPDT). Certified consultants must meet a number of rigorous requirements, including three to five years of experience working with behavioral issues in dogs, successful completion of a national exam in behavioral science and learning theory, and continuing education every year to make sure their knowledge stays current.

Certified behavior consultants have the initials CDBC (Certified Dog Behavior Consultant) or CBCC-KA (Certified Behavior Consultant Canine-Knowledge Assessed) after their name. Both the IAABC (www.iaabc.org) and CCPDT (www.ccpdt.org) have directories that you can search to find a consultant in your area.

4 ▸ DOG TRAINERS

As the name implies, dog trainers generally teach basic obedience skills and puppy socialization classes, and troubleshoot simple behavioral issues like jumping on people or pulling on the leash. Some may specialize in dog sports like agility or rally obedience, and others may train dogs to give them specific skills for therapy or service work.

Although some trainers may be quite knowledgeable about behavioral issues in dogs, others may not have much experience or education in how to manage serious behavioral problems. If you opt to work with a trainer rather than a credentialed behavioral professional, make sure you do your homework.

Ask about their certifications and professional memberships and what they do to stay current in the field. A reputable trainer will be happy to share this information with you. Independent certifications such as a CPDT-KA (Certified Professional Dog Trainer-Knowledge Assessed) or CPDT-KSA (Certified Professional Dog Trainer-Knowledge and Skills Assessed) are a good sign, as is membership in professional organizations like the Association of Professional Dog Trainers (APDT) or the Pet Professional Guild (PPG).

A skilled trainer can be tremendously helpful, but a poor training experience can harm your dog and worsen his behavioral issues. Don't be afraid to ask questions, and be sure to choose someone you feel you can trust.

AGGRESSION TO VISITORS

If you've ever had a dog who barks and growls at unfamiliar people when they come to visit, you know how challenging this problem can be. It's stressful for owners, scary for guests, and can be very dangerous if your dog's behavior ever escalates to biting.

So why do some dogs do this?

Aggressive behavior toward strangers is generally caused by fear. Dogs who act this way are anxious and uncomfortable around people they don't know, so they bark, growl, and may even bite in an effort to protect themselves. This tendency toward fearfulness can be caused by genetics, negative early experiences, or a lack of proper socialization during puppyhood.

Treatment for this problem involves environmental management to keep everyone safe, as well as reward-based training. Your goal is to address your dog's fear and teach him that strangers aren't so scary.

Managing Aggression Toward Visitors

To manage your dog's aggression toward visitors:

1 ▸ ASK VISITORS TO CALL BEFORE COMING OVER

Having advance notice before people arrive at your home allows you plan ahead and take appropriate precautions to keep everyone safe.

2 ▸ CONFINE YOUR DOG BEFORE THEY ARRIVE

Put him in his crate or in a separate room with the door closed before any guests enter the house. You can give him a special treat such as a pig ear, bully stick, or a Kong stuffed with peanut butter to help keep him busy.

3 ▸ KEEP EVERYONE SEPARATED DURING THE VISIT

Make sure your dog stays in his crate or "safe room" until after your guests have left. This prevents any problems from occurring, and this also keeps the aggressive behavior from getting worse.

DOG TRAINING TIP

You might be tempted to let your dog continue to meet visitors in the hopes that he will eventually get used to them so that his aggression resolves itself on its own. Unfortunately, this rarely happens. Instead, it's more likely that your dog's behavior will get worse over time. It's far more helpful to avoid any contact with visitors unless you are actively working on the problem. This approach is much safer and less stressful for both you and your dog.

AGGRESSION TO VISITORS—TRAINING

If your dog has ever bitten anyone, or if you are concerned that he might, muzzle training (covered in Part III) is highly recommended for safety reasons before moving forward with this training plan. The use of a muzzle is to prevent any accidental bites from occurring, in case something unexpected happens or your dog gets spooked during the training session.

Training Your Dog to Be Less Aggressive to Visitors

To train your dog to be less aggressive to visitors:

1 ▸ ENLIST A HELPER

You will need an assistant who your dog doesn't know well to act as a "visitor" for your first few training sessions. You may have a friend or relative who is willing to help. It's important not to use a real-life visitor at first. At this stage, you need a helper who will follow your instructions; this allows you to control the situation to help ensure that your dog is successful.

2 ▸ CONFINE YOUR DOG

Put your dog in his crate or safe room before your helper arrives, just as you would with any other guest.

3 ▸ LET YOUR HELPER COME IN AND GET SEATED

Once everything is calm, you can bring out your dog on a leash. Make sure he's wearing his muzzle for safety, if needed.

4 ▸ KEEP YOUR DISTANCE

Stand across the room from your helper, as far away as possible. Keep your dog with you on-leash so that he can't go any closer. You want to keep your dog far enough away that he can be calm and take treats from you without getting upset.

Your helper should sit quietly during this process, without speaking to your dog or making eye contact.

5 ▸ REWARD YOUR DOG

Every time your dog looks at the helper, praise and reward him with a treat. For best results, use very high-value rewards. Most dogs do well with lunch meat, cheese, or hot dogs.

Your goal with this exercise is to teach your dog that seeing visitors equals yummy treats. Over time, he will become less and less afraid and will even look forward to having people visit.

If your dog barks or growls, don't scold him. Remember that he's anxious; punishment will only make things worse. Just move a bit farther away to make him more comfortable and continue feeding treats.

6 ▸ KEEP IT SHORT AND SWEET

Continue this procedure for two to three minutes, then take your dog back to his safe room. As long as things are going well, you can repeat this several times in a single training session if you wish.

7 ▸ START MOVING CLOSER

Once your dog is eagerly glancing at the helper and then back at you for his treat with no growling or barking at all, you can gradually begin moving closer. Work your way across the room until your dog can be right beside your helper without any signs of anxiety.

This may take anywhere from a single session to several weeks, or even months—every dog is different. So be patient, and take things as slowly as needed.

8 ▸ DO IT ALL AGAIN WITH SOMEONE NEW

Repeat steps 1–7 with another helper, if possible. Some dogs may need to do this a few times with different people before they're ready to move on.

9 ▸ TRY THE REAL THING

Eventually, you can use this same procedure to bring your dog out when you have real-life visitors in the house.

If your dog seems completely comfortable on-leash taking treats, you can try allowing him some free time in the house when people are visiting. Make sure to monitor him closely for any signs of stress, and take him back to his safe room if you have any concerns.

DOG TRAINING TIP

With lots of practice, some fear-aggressive dogs will eventually become comfortable enough to be loose in the house when visitors are around—at least with small groups and relatively quiet gatherings. Other dogs may never get to this point, and may need to be kept separated from strangers at all times unless they are on-leash and under control.

If you have trouble making progress or have any safety concerns with your dog's training plan, it's always best to consult a qualified behavioral professional for help.

AGGRESSION TO UNFAMILIAR DOGS

Some dogs (like some people) are easy-going extroverts who get along with everyone. Big or small, calm or playful, they're happy to make friends with any dog they meet. These are the social butterflies of the canine world who often enjoy daycare and dog parks, and they can be trusted to say hello to another dog on a walk without any problems.

If this sounds like your dog, great. Relax, count your blessings, and feel free to skip this section.

But what if your dog is more selective about which dogs he likes? Or worse, what if he barks and lunges, or even gets into fights with other dogs every time he meets one?

First of all, don't feel bad—you're not alone. Aggressive behavior toward strange dogs is a common problem, and one that's often very manageable with a good training plan. Treatment for this issue normally involves reward-based training to teach your dog to be calm and friendly with other dogs, as well as learning to avoid situations that are likely to cause problems.

THREE STEPS TO
Managing Aggression to Unfamiliar Dogs

To manage aggression toward unfamiliar dogs:

1 ▸ FIRST, DOES YOUR DOG REALLY HAVE A PROBLEM?

An occasional skirmish with another dog at the park or during rowdy play is normal and expected, just as young children may sometimes get into minor fights on the playground. Normal dog "arguments" are often noisy and dramatic, with lots of snarling and snapping.

Your dog may snap or growl at another dog who is rude during their initial meeting or who is too rough or pushy during play. This is a normal part of canine communication. The other dog should take the hint and back off. Your dog should also relax and move on without becoming overly upset.

But what if your dog always becomes aggressive as soon as he meets another dog, or gets into frequent fights at the park without any obvious trigger? In that case, it's more likely that your dog has a problem. He may be uncomfortable around other dogs due to a lack of early socialization or a previous bad experience, or he may simply have poor social skills and not know what else to do. Either way, he definitely needs some guidance.

2 ▸ IDENTIFY LIKELY TRIGGERS FOR YOUR DOG

Does he get into fights every time he's in a play group, or does he fight only if there are toys or treats involved? Perhaps he does well with small dogs or dogs who are calm and laid-back but gets defensive and upset with larger or more energetic playmates. In severe cases, your dog may become aggressive every time he meets another dog, regardless of the situation. Whatever your dog's triggers are, you need to know them so that you can address them appropriately. If your dog is only aggressive to other dogs when he is on-leash, see Leash Reactivity later in this part for more information on how to manage this problem.

3 ▸ AVOID TROUBLE WHENEVER YOU CAN

This might mean staying away from the dog park if there are large dogs or rough players there, or in some cases avoiding it altogether. Or it may mean removing toys from the area and putting away any treats before allowing your dog off-leash to play. The bottom line is this: if you know that your dog is likely to be aggressive in any given situation, don't risk it. Better to walk away and avoid the problem than risk making things worse.

DOG TRAINING TIP

Many owners mistakenly believe that their aggressive dog will become "socialized" if they continue taking him to the park and letting him interact with other dogs. Unfortunately, this couldn't be further from the truth. In most cases, this plan backfires spectacularly and the aggression gets worse over time. It also puts your dog, and other dogs, at risk of being injured if a fight occurs.

If you have any concerns at all that your dog may be aggressive, keep him away from chaotic situations like this with dogs you don't know. You'll have much more success working on the problem using a step-by-step, carefully controlled training plan.

SIX STEPS TO

Train Your Dog to Be Less Aggressive to Unfamiliar Dogs

To train your dog to be less aggressive to unfamiliar dogs:

1 ▸ DECIDE IF YOU WANT TO TRAIN VERSUS MANAGE

I know, I know—this seems like an odd first step, doesn't it? But the truth is, there's nothing wrong with simply avoiding dog parks or play groups with strange dogs if your dog doesn't handle them well. If he's happy and well-adjusted most of the time and only becomes aggressive in uncontrolled off-leash situations like this, you don't necessarily need to "fix" anything. Just enjoy your dog for who he is, and let him keep to himself.

2 ▸ IF YOU WANT TO WORK ON THINGS, GREAT!

You'll need some tasty treats and an organized training plan. Don't be afraid to consult a professional for help getting started.

3 ▸ START OUT WITH WHAT YOUR DOG CAN HANDLE

This means exposing him to his trigger situations in small doses, with lots of rewards for staying calm.

For example: if he has trouble in play groups, try letting him play for thirty seconds, then calling him back for a reward and a chance to calm down. This keeps his arousal level low so that he's less likely to get upset, and it ensures that he gets lots of rewards for playing nicely.

If he's aggressive toward other dogs on-leash, practice with a friendly, easy-going "helper dog" who won't get upset. Praise and reward your dog for looking calmly at him from a distance, gradually getting closer over time.

4 ▸ WORK UP SLOWLY TO REAL-LIFE SITUATIONS

Increase his exposure to other dogs over time, as long as things are going well.

In a play group, allow him to play for sixty seconds at a time before calling him back for a reward. Then ninety seconds, then two minutes, and so on. Eventually, you can work up to allowing him to play uninterrupted, provided that everyone is getting along.

On-leash, you can allow him to approach and greet the other dog as long as he is able to do this calmly. Working with a trainer on this can be very helpful, especially if you're unsure about reading his body language for signs of stress or tension.

5 ▸ KEEP A CLOSE EYE ON YOUR DOG

If he stiffens up, growls, or tries to fight, this is a sign that you may have pushed things too far, too quickly. Get him out of the situation as quickly as you can, and praise and reward once he's calm again. This happens sometimes, so don't give up. Just back up to the last point where your dog was successful, and start again from there.

6 ▸ STAY VIGILANT

Assuming that all goes well, your dog may eventually be able to interact normally with other dogs in situations that would have been a problem in the past. If you get to this point, great job! But keep in mind that behavioral issues are rarely "cured." You will always need to monitor your dog closely and be ready to remove him from the situation if any problems arise.

AGGRESSION BETWEEN DOGS IN THE SAME HOUSEHOLD

As anyone who lives in a multi-dog household can attest, occasional squabbles between canine family members are common. Dogs may growl, show their teeth, and even snarl or snap at one another from time to time as a way of settling mild disagreements over chew toys or comfy resting spots. This is part of normal canine communication, just like human siblings argue over similar problems. But when does this type of conflict cross the line into serious aggression that needs to be addressed?

If you have two (or more) dogs who regularly get into fights that require human intervention to stop, or if your dog has ever injured one of his housemates during an altercation, this isn't normal. Unfortunately, the problem is likely to get worse over time if you don't take action.

For mild to moderate aggression issues between family dogs, a smart management plan can often be enough to restore harmony in the household. There are some simple changes you can make to your daily routine to help prevent conflict and diffuse tense situations before they escalate—you just need to be proactive and learn to plan ahead to help avoid problems.

THREE STEPS TO
Manage a Problem with Inter-Dog Aggression

To manage problems with inter-dog aggression:

1 ▸ AVOID COMMON TRIGGERS FOR FIGHTS

This might sound difficult at first, but the truth is, most cases of aggression between dogs in a household occur over a handful of predictable scenarios that can often be avoided with a little foresight. You should:

- Feed your dogs in separate rooms or secure areas (such as in their crates) to avoid competition over food. Keep everyone separated until all dogs are finished eating and the empty bowls are put away.

- Keep chew toys or other high-value items (bully sticks, rawhides, etc.) put away, and only give them when the dogs are in their crates or in separate rooms.

- During times of high excitement, such as when dinner is being prepared or when visitors are entering the house, keep the dogs away from the action by using a baby gate or other barrier, or put them in a separate room until things calm down.

- Monitor play to ensure that your dogs aren't becoming overly excited or "wound-up," as over-arousal can often spill over into fighting if it isn't interrupted. Practice calling the dogs over to you during high-intensity play for praise and treats to help calm things down, then release them back to their game once everyone is under control.

2 ▶ SEPARATE YOUR DOGS WHEN NEEDED

If you have any concerns that your dogs may get into a serious fight while you're not home, or if you're busy and can't watch them, put them in their crates or in separate rooms to make sure that everyone stays safe.

3 ▶ IF YOU SEE SIGNS OF TENSION, INTERVENE

Most dogs will give some warning signs prior to starting a fight with a housemate. These signs can include freezing, giving a hard stare, growling, or showing teeth. If you see trouble brewing, change the subject by calling everyone over for a treat or asking if they want to go for a walk. Often, redirects like these work well to diffuse the situation and can be very effective at preventing problems.

As tempting as it might be, don't punish your dog for growling or giving other warning signs. Although it may temporarily seem to work by suppressing the unwanted behavior, you run the risk of making things worse over time by making your dogs even more tense around each other and teaching them to attack without warning in the future.

DOG TRAINING TIP

If your dogs are intact males, consider having them neutered. Although this doesn't always resolve aggression issues, we know that intact males are more likely to have trouble getting along with each other as compared to neutered males or male/female pairs. With females, spaying is not as likely to be helpful unless the aggression mainly occurs during heat cycles, when some female dogs are more temperamental and "grumpier" than normal.

AGGRESSIVE DOGS WHO'VE BEEN SEPARATED

With severe inter-dog aggression, it may be necessary to completely separate both dogs and do a gradual reintroduction after several days or weeks to try and teach them to coexist peacefully again. If you find yourself in this position, getting in touch with a qualified trainer for some hands-on guidance is always recommended.

These are difficult situations, and there may be cases where the dogs in question are simply not able to live together without problems. A veterinary behaviorist or other professional can evaluate your dogs in person to help you set realistic goals for what can be accomplished.

Reintroduce Aggressive Dogs Who've Been Separated

The following training plan should be considered a general guideline for reintroducing a pair of aggressive dogs who have been separated:

1 ▸ START WITH BOTH DOGS ON-LEASH

You will need a helper for this plan, since each dog needs to be held by a separate person. You will also need a large open space to work in. This could be a room in the house such as a playroom or basement, or you can work outside in the yard if you prefer.

Each handler should have a good supply of tasty treats—high-value food like chicken, roast beef, or hot dog slices usually works best for this exercise.

2 ▸ KEEP LOTS OF DISTANCE

Bring both dogs into the working area, on opposite sides. You want to put lots of distance between them at first. Each person should praise and reward his/her dog each time the dogs look at each other. Do this for three to five minutes, giving lots of treats for calm behavior, then end the session.

Ideally, the dogs should be far enough apart so that they can look at each other calmly, focus on their handlers, and take treats. If either of the dogs becomes aggressive and begins barking or lunging, or is too nervous or upset to take treats, this means that you need more distance. You may need to find a larger area to work in.

3 ▸ MAKE SURE BOTH DOGS ARE RELAXED AND HAPPY

Repeat step 2 several times. The goal here is to teach both dogs to associate good things with seeing each other. Be sure to establish a strong foundation of calm, relaxed behavior before attempting to go any further.

4 ▸ CLOSE THE GAP

When both dogs eagerly look at each other and then back at their handler for treats, with no growling or barking at all, you can gradually begin allowing them to move closer together. Do this very slowly, one tiny step at a time—don't rush!

DOG TRAINING TIP

If either of the dogs has a history of causing injuries during fights, or if you are concerned that this may happen, consider muzzle training for one or both dogs before attempting to reintroduce them. The muzzle acts as a "safety belt" to help ensure that no one gets hurt in the event of a problem, but you will still need to go through the training process slowly and carefully. See Part III for more detailed instructions on training your dog to wear a muzzle comfortably.

5 ▸ CONTINUE REWARDING FOR CALM BEHAVIOR

Eventually, you can work your way up to having the dogs side by side, still on-leash and under control to prevent any problems. Make sure to praise and reward both dogs generously for remaining calm and relaxed, and be on the lookout for any signs of tension. If you have any concerns, back up and increase the distance between them for the next few sessions.

6 ▸ TRY IT OFF-LEASH

Once the dogs are showing only casual interest in each other during your training sessions, you can try allowing them off-leash together for a few minutes at a time. Work up to longer periods of being loose together as long as things are going well, and be ready to separate them again if needed. Achieving a permanent "fix" can be difficult in serious cases of housemate aggression, so continued vigilance is important.

OWNER-DIRECTED AGGRESSION

Few things are as upsetting (and as unexpected, in most cases) as being bitten by your own dog. This happens more often than you might think, so don't take it personally.

Dogs may show aggression toward their owners or family members for a variety of reasons. In some situations, growling, snapping, or even biting can be a normal response to being hurt or frightened. For example, your dog may instinctively turn and snap at you if you accidentally step on his tail. Most of us would agree that this is understandable and is not necessarily cause for alarm.

However, what if your dog is growling or even biting you over more trivial things: basic handling or grooming, walking by the food bowl while he's eating, or sitting down near him on the couch? Such behavior is much more concerning. Aggression over normal, everyday activities can be a significant safety issue as well as a strain on your relationship with your dog, so it's well worth addressing this behavior.

Like other types of aggressive behavior in dogs, owner-directed aggression is best handled with a combination of smart management to help avoid problems and a good training plan to teach more desired behavior.

FOUR STEPS TO
Handle Owner-Directed Aggression

To safely manage a problem with owner-directed aggression:

1 ▸ IDENTIFY AND AVOID TRIGGERS

Whenever possible, avoid interactions that are likely to result in aggressive behavior from your dog. Depending on your pup's specific issues, high-risk situations might include the following:

- Disturbing your dog while he is sleeping or resting
- Approaching him while he's eating or chewing on a special treat or toy
- Grabbing or reaching for his collar
- Physically restraining, lifting, or carrying your dog
- Performing grooming tasks like brushing or nail trimming

2 ▸ WORK ON REWARD-BASED OBEDIENCE TRAINING

While training will not resolve an aggression problem on its own, teaching your dog some obedience skills will improve your ability to communicate with him and will allow you to ask him to do things safely.

3 ▸ BE POSITIVE AND CONSISTENT

Ask your dog to perform a simple trick or obedience behavior prior to putting his food bowl down, attaching his leash to go for a walk, and so forth. By keeping your interactions with your dog as consistent and predictable as possible, you can greatly reduce the risk of aggressive behavior. If he knows how to get what he wants by behaving nicely, he will learn that he doesn't need to snap or bite.

4 ▶ DON'T PUNISH

As tempting as it might be, don't punish your dog for aggressive behavior or use any correction-based training methods for his obedience training. Punishment (including verbal scolding, leash corrections, shock collars, and the like) often makes dogs frustrated and defensive, which can lead to worsening of the aggression over time. Instead, focus on teaching your pup what you want him to do, and reward him for cooperating.

DOG TRAINING TIP

Contrary to popular belief, owner-directed aggression has nothing to do with dominance or who is "alpha" in the relationship between you and your dog. Most dogs who bite their owners are acting this way because they are defensive and insecure, and they often overreact with aggression when they don't know what else to do.

For this reason, treatment is teaching your dog to respond to these challenges in a more positive way. This requires consistency, patience, and trust. Training techniques that use force or intimidation such as stare-downs, "alpha rolls," scruffing, or harsh verbal corrections should be strictly avoided, as they tend to be counterproductive and can dramatically increase the risk of a bite.

OWNER-DIRECTED AGGRESSION—TRIGGERS

Most dogs who show aggression toward their owners have a small number of fairly predictable triggers that may cause them to growl or snap. While avoiding these situations as much as possible is a good starting point, this isn't always practical.

Fortunately, with a little time and effort, you can address this behavior through training. This generally involves using rewards to help your dog stay calm and relaxed during these "high-risk" interactions, as well as teaching some specific obedience cues to make things easier.

Countering Owner-Directed Aggression—Triggers

Here are some specific training solutions for each of the trigger situations mentioned previously. As always, if you run into problems or have any concerns for your safety, don't hesitate to find a professional who can help you in person. The following steps outline what to do when you are:

1 ▸ DISTURBING YOUR DOG WHILE HE'S SLEEPING OR RESTING

- Teach your dog the "off" command, as described in Part II. If he's resting on the couch or bed and you need him to move, tell him, "Off." Then, once he's down, praise and reward him with a treat.
- The "touch" command can also be very useful for moving your dog around without needing to physically push him or grab his collar. See Six Steps to Training "Touch" (Hand Target) in Part II.
- If needed, you can also have your dog wear a drag line (a lightweight leash) in the house while you're working on this problem. This can be used to help move him from one place to another in a pinch—just pick up the line near the end, well away from your dog, and use it to physically guide him where you need him to go. This is much safer than trying to grab his collar or touch his body. Make sure to praise and reward when he does what you ask, even if you had to help him a bit.

2 ▶ APPROACHING YOUR DOG WHILE HE'S EATING OR CHEWING ON A SPECIAL TREAT OR TOY

- Work with your pup on the "drop it" command, as described in Part II. This training often helps dogs learn to be less defensive about their things and gives you a safe way to get something away from him if needed.

- You can also use rewards to teach your dog to associate your approaches to him with good things. For example, if he growls when you walk past his food bowl, start by standing at a distance and tossing pieces of cheese or hot dog slices into his bowl while he eats. As long as he's calm and relaxed, you can gradually move closer over the course of several sessions, until you can walk all the way up to his bowl, drop in a treat, and walk away while your pup happily wags his tail.

- This same procedure can be used if your dog doesn't like being approached while he's chewing on a rawhide or is playing with one of his toys.

3 ▶ GRABBING OR REACHING FOR YOUR DOG'S COLLAR

- Sit down with your dog and a handful of tasty treats. Practice lightly touching your dog's head or back at first, if he's already anxious about having his collar handled. Praise and reward with a treat after every touch.

- Once he's comfortable having you touch his body, begin gradually moving closer to the collar. First touch his neck or chest, then praise and reward. Repeat this several times.

- Next, lightly touch his collar, then immediately praise and give a treat. Practice this until he's happy and relaxed. Work your way up to gently closing your fingers around his collar, giving a treat, and letting go.

- Finally, try reaching for his collar "out of the blue" at random times around the house. As before, make sure you praise and reward with a treat each time. With practice, your dog will begin to look forward to having you grab his collar since it always predicts good things.

4 ▸ PHYSICALLY RESTRAINING, LIFTING, OR CARRYING YOUR DOG

- Teach your dog to go where you ask him to, rather than picking him up or carrying him. This is an easy way to avoid problems if your dog is uncomfortable being held.
- Most dogs can easily learn to hop into the car, go into their crate, or hold still for an exam without difficulty. See the sections Nine Steps to Get Over Car-Ride Anxiety, Seven Steps to Crate Training, and Six Steps to Standing Still for a Physical Exam for details on teaching these skills.

5 ▸ PERFORMING GROOMING TASKS LIKE BRUSHING OR NAIL TRIMMING

- Teach your dog to stand calmly for basic handling and grooming tasks. With training, most dogs can learn to cooperate happily with these procedures rather than struggling and becoming aggressive.
- See Part III for detailed instructions on how to teach your dog to stay calm and relaxed for brushing, nail trimming, dental care, and the like.

DOG TRAINING TIP

If your dog has ever bitten you, or if you have concerns that he might, consider teaching him to wear a muzzle prior to attempting any of the training projects discussed here. You will still need to proceed slowly and make sure to keep your dog comfortable at every step, but the muzzle can help make sure that everyone stays safe if something unexpected happens.

PREDATORY AGGRESSION

We all know, intellectually, that dogs are descended from wild predators that had to hunt and kill in order to survive—though it's hard to remember this sometimes. When your pup is snuggled up against you with his head in your lap, snoring on the couch, he can seem so far removed from a wild wolf or coyote as to render the comparison moot.

The truth is, though, that even the most pampered of pets can still retain the neurological "hard wiring" needed to recognize prey animals and chase them down. If you've ever seen your dog catch sight of a squirrel on a walk or run loose in an open field, then you know the pattern. Initially, most dogs will freeze—a hard, focused stare, mouth closed, ears forward.

What happens next depends on the dog.

Some dogs enjoy the thrill of the chase and nothing else. But others will go through the entire sequence of grabbing, shaking, and killing their prey, whether it's a wild animal like a squirrel or a house pet such as a cat or smaller dog. This type of predatory behavior is especially common in sighthounds, terriers, and northern breeds such as Siberian huskies and Alaskan malamutes, but it can occur in individuals of any breed.

If your dog has a history of chasing, attacking, or even killing cats or other small animals, what can you do? For starters, you'll need to take precautions to keep other animals safe.

THREE STEPS TO

Control Predatory Aggression Toward Smaller Animals

To safely manage a dog with predatory aggression toward smaller animals:

1 ▸ KEEP HOUSE PETS SAFELY SEPARATED

In the house, keep cats or smaller dogs in a separate room with the door closed. When smaller animals are loose in the house, your dog should be held on-leash so that you can prevent any problems.

This is critically important, because chasing other animals is a very self-reinforcing behavior! The more your dog practices trying to catch his "prey," the stronger and more entrenched this behavior will become. So make sure that he doesn't get the chance to do it, even when you're not actively working on training.

2 ▸ ALWAYS USE A LEASH

Outside, keep your dog safely on-leash in any areas where you may encounter a neighbor's pets or wild animals such as rabbits or squirrels. Even if your dog is usually reliable about coming back when you call him, he may not respond if he's in the middle of a chase.

3 ▸ TRY OTHER TOOLS IF NEEDED

Consider using a head halter such as a Halti or Gentle Leader for better control of your dog if you will be in close quarters with other animals. A muzzle can also be a good option, either in the house or on walks. See Eight Steps to Muzzle Training in Part III for instructions on teaching your dog to wear a muzzle comfortably.

Train Against Predatory Aggression

The basic approach to training against predatory aggression involves teaching your dog to voluntarily "check in" with you for a treat whenever he sees another animal. This is an effective way of interrupting the predatory sequence before he becomes too intently focused to respond.

Most dogs with this problem can make significant improvements, but realistic goals will vary depending on the situation. For example, most dogs can learn to safely go for neighborhood leash walks where smaller dogs are also present on-leash. But if your pup has a history of chasing or killing small animals, it may never be safe to take him to the dog park and turn him loose to run with Chihuahuas and Yorkies in the same area.

When in doubt, always err on the side of safety. It only takes a moment for tragedy to strike, and this type of behavior can have severe legal consequences for you if an accident does happen.

To train your dog to stop chasing other animals:

1 ▸ USE YOUR LEASH

Keep your dog on-leash at all times during training. You can work on this issue anytime you're going to be sitting in one place for a while. Evening "downtime" while watching TV is a perfect time for this training.

2 ▸ BIDE YOUR TIME

Wait for a smaller animal to come into view. If needed, in certain situations you can use a baby gate or other barrier at first to prevent the smaller animals from approaching too closely.

3 ▸ REWARD YOUR DOG

As soon as your dog notices the other animal, immediately praise and reward. Use very tasty treats for this exercise, since this is challenging for most dogs. Cheese, chicken, or roast beef are usually good choices.

4 ▸ REPEAT STEP 3 SEVERAL TIMES

Your dog should start to glance at the other animal, then look expectantly at you for his treat. This is exactly what you want to see, so praise and reward generously when it happens.

5 ▸ KEEP PRACTICING

Continue working on this skill until your dog automatically looks up at you, without any prompting, as soon as he notices the other animal. This may take one or two sessions, several days, or several weeks depending on the dog. Remember to be patient, and don't rush.

6 ▸ TRY IT OFF-LEASH

At this point, you can begin allowing your dog to be off-leash during your training sessions. Make sure to keep your leash and treats handy! By now, he should be good at interrupting himself and checking in with you whenever he sees a smaller animal, be it a squirrel, cat, or other dog. Praise and reward every time, as before.

7 ▸ CUT BACK ON THE TREATS

Eventually, as this behavior becomes more and more automatic and chasing becomes less of a habit, you should be able to reward less frequently. With some dogs, you may be able to fade out treats entirely, while other dogs will need frequent rewards to remind them of what you want.

Control Aggression on Walks

To control aggression on walks:

1 ▸ BE PREPARED

Carry a good supply of tasty treats with you whenever you walk your dog.

2 ▸ WAIT FOR AN OPPORTUNITY

As soon as your dog notices another animal (such as a cat, rabbit, or squirrel), praise and reward with a treat.

3 ▸ REPEAT STEP 2 SEVERAL TIMES

With practice, your dog will start to look up at you automatically as soon as he notices a potential "prey" animal to chase. Reward generously when he does this.

4 ▸ BACK AWAY IF NEEDED

You may notice that, at times, your dog becomes fixated on the other animal and can't be distracted, even with treats. This is very common, so don't worry. If this happens, it means that your dog needs more distance. Try backing away several feet, bringing him with you on-leash, until he breaks his focus and looks back at you. Praise and reward him, as usual.

5 ▸ KEEP YOUR DISTANCE

Stay as far away from other animals as possible in the early stages of training, as this will help your dog be successful. Of course this isn't always possible, so if you're surprised by a "too close" cat or squirrel, just back up until your dog can focus again. He'll get better at this with practice, so don't give up.

6 ▸ ENJOY YOUR WALKS!

Eventually, you'll find that you can walk your dog past other animals while he looks happily at you for his treat. Congratulate yourself when you're able to do this. For most prey-driven dogs, it takes lots of time and patience to get there.

RESOURCE GUARDING

As you've probably noticed if you're a dog owner, especially if you have multiple pets, most dogs don't like to share. When they're enjoying their dinner, chewing on a tasty rawhide, or playing with their favorite squeaky toy, they may not be interested in letting anyone else in on the action. This guarding often takes the form of growling, snarling, snapping, or even biting, which can be alarming for many pet parents.

So first things first. It might surprise you to learn that to some extent, resource guarding is perfectly normal behavior. Even though most of our pet pups today live pampered lives, remember that they're descended from wild animals and street dogs who have evolved in a much harsher world.

In the wild, a dog who doesn't protect his food from other animals goes hungry. Because of this, the instinctive drive to guard valuable resources such as treats, toys, and food is a strong one—even in pet dogs, who no longer need this particular behavior pattern as much as they once did. Unfortunately, this can sometimes lead to problems if your pup won't let you walk past his dinner bowl without growling or gets into fights with his doggy housemates over toys or treats.

Because this behavior is so strongly hard-wired in many dogs, a smart management plan is often the simplest option if your pup has a tendency to guard things. This doesn't mean "avoiding the problem"; it just means respecting the fact that he might need more space to feel comfortable when he's eating or chewing on his favorite bone.

Manage Resource Guarding

To safely manage a problem with resource guarding:

1 ▸ LEAVE YOUR DOG ALONE WHILE HE'S EATING

Put his food bowl down and walk away, and don't disturb him again until he's completely finished.

If you have young children or other pets in the house, it's best to feed your dog in a separate room with the door closed to prevent any problems. Once he's finished eating, you can let him out and put away the empty bowl.

2 ▸ CONFINE YOUR DOG WITH CHEW TOYS

Only give valuable chew treats, like rawhides or bully sticks, when your dog is in his crate or in a separate room.

3 ▸ AVOID POTENTIAL PROBLEMS WITH OTHER DOGS

Put away toys and treats during playtime, or when another dog is nearby.

4 ▸ TRADE FOR A TREAT IF NEEDED

If you need to get something away from your dog, like a stolen item from the trash can, use a tasty treat to "trade." This is much safer than attempting to forcibly take the item away. To do this effectively:

- Grab a piece of cheese or chicken from the refrigerator, or get a handful of his favorite dog treats.
- Call your dog's name and show him the treat. If you've chosen something tasty enough, he should be very interested.
- Toss your treat on the floor a few feet away. Most dogs will let go of the item they're holding and run over to get the treat. You should be able to safely pick up the item and put it away while he's busy eating.

ELEVEN STEPS TO
Train Against Resource Guarding

For dogs with more severe resource guarding issues, or in situations where management alone may not be practical as a long-term solution, training can be very helpful.

In order to make lasting changes in your dog's resource guarding behavior, you need to teach him to feel differently about having you approach him when he has something valuable. You want him to brighten up and be happy that you're coming over, rather than to get tense and defensive.

This means going very slowly and using lots of rewards to help him associate good things with having humans approach during mealtimes, or while he's enjoying a tasty bone on the couch.

To teach your dog not to guard things from you:

1 ▶ GIVE HIM PLENTY OF SPACE

Stand at a distance from your dog while he's eating and have a handful of tasty treats ready. (You can use this same basic approach when your dog is guarding other things as well, such as chew items or toys.) Make sure that the treat you're using is something exciting, like roast beef or hot dog slices; your treats should be much tastier than what your dog already has.

Note that your starting distance should be far enough away that he can comfortably ignore you. If he seems tense or worried about your presence, this means you're too close. Back up until he's not paying any attention to you at all.

2 ▸ TOSS TREATS FROM A DISTANCE

Without moving any closer, toss a treat so that it lands beside him. He should eat it eagerly, then go back to his dinner.

3 ▸ REPEAT STEP 2 SEVERAL TIMES

Continue doing this until you've tossed your entire handful of treats—at least ten to fifteen treats per session is best. When you're done, walk away and leave your dog alone to finish eating.

4 ▸ KEEP AN EYE ON YOUR DOG

Repeat this process at each mealtime, paying close attention to your dog's body language. After a few sessions, he should start to look happy when he notices you standing nearby. Look for a quick tail wag or a "perking up" of his ears. He should look eager, as if he's waiting for his treats. This is exactly what you want. At this point, you're ready to begin slowly moving closer.

5 ▸ STEP A BIT CLOSER

The next time you practice, try standing one step nearer to your dog while he eats. Repeat steps 2 and 3, as before.

6 ▸ CONTINUE CLOSING THE GAP

At every step, make sure that your dog seems completely relaxed and comfortable before moving any closer. This may take days, weeks, or even months depending on the dog. Be patient and don't rush things.

7 ▸ STAND BESIDE THE BOWL

Eventually, after many sessions of practicing and gradually moving closer, you should be able to stand right beside your dog's bowl while he's eating.

8 ▸ ADD A TREAT TO HIS DINNER

As long as he seems happy and relaxed, bend down to drop a treat into his bowl while he's eating. Repeat this ten to fifteen times, as before, then walk away and leave him alone to finish.

If your dog has ever bitten you over food, or if you're concerned that he might, do not attempt this step without some in-person guidance from a professional. He/she can help you make sure you're reading your dog's body language correctly so as to prevent any unexpected problems.

9 ▸ PRACTICE TO BUILD CONFIDENCE

Repeat step 8 several times during different training sessions to ensure that your dog is completely comfortable before moving on.

10 ▸ PICK UP THE BOWL

If you wish, you can progress to picking up your dog's bowl, adding a handful of treats, and immediately giving it back. This teaches your dog that great things happen when you take his food away: not only will he get it back, but he'll get a bonus too.

> **DOG TRAINING TIP**
>
> Training techniques that involve force or intimidation, or taking away food or toys from your dog, are *never* recommended for resource guarding. Although they may seem to work temporarily by suppressing your dog's warning signals, they only teach your dog to be more fearful and defensive when you approach him.

11 ▸ TRY IT WITH SOMEONE NEW

Repeat steps 1–10 with each family member separately, if needed. Dogs don't always generalize well, so even though he might be fine with you approaching his bowl, he may still guard it from your spouse or other humans in your home.

LEASH REACTIVITY

If you have a hard time walking your dog because he barks at things (usually people or other dogs), don't worry—you're definitely not alone. Leash reactivity is a very common problem for many pet dogs, and one that's usually very treatable with a good training plan.

Most reactive dogs act this way for one of two reasons:

- They may be fearful of unfamiliar people or other dogs, which can happen as a result of poor socialization or negative early experiences, or this can simply be a result of genetics.
- They may be overly friendly and excited, which causes them to bark and pull on the leash whenever they see someone they want to say hello to. These dogs are often referred to as "frustrated greeters."

Fortunately, regardless of which category your dog falls into, the approach to training and management for this problem is the same. It's all about managing the environment so that you set your dog up for success, rewarding for the behavior you want, and gradually making things more challenging as long as he's doing well.

Manage Leash Reactivity

To manage a problem with leash reactivity:

1 ▶ PLAN YOUR WALKS STRATEGICALLY

Take your dog for walks during quiet times of the day when other people and dogs are less likely to be out. This might mean very early in the morning or late at night before bed. You'll be much more relaxed if you're not constantly worried about running into someone whom your dog may bark at, which means a more pleasant walk for both of you.

If the streets around your house are generally too busy for your dog, you could also drive someplace else to walk him—perhaps a park or a quieter neighborhood nearby.

2 ▶ REDIRECT AND LEAVE AS NEEDED

Carry treats with you on walks, and practice redirecting your dog and walking away to avoid problems when necessary.

If you see another person or dog approaching in the distance, hold a treat in front of your dog's nose to get his attention. Then turn around and walk in the opposite direction. Praise and reward your dog for coming with you. This allows you to keep a safe distance from things that your dog may bark at if you were to encounter them unexpectedly.

3 ▸ USE A HALTER FOR MORE CONTROL

Consider using a head halter such as a Halti or Gentle Leader, especially if you have trouble controlling your dog or redirecting his attention when he gets upset.

Although these tools can look intimidating at first, they don't hurt your dog or restrict his mouth at all. Instead, they work like a halter for a horse, giving you control of your dog's head. This makes it much easier to turn him toward you and lead him away if you run into problems.

SEVEN STEPS TO

Train Against Leash Reactivity

Management is a great starting point, and it's definitely necessary in the early stages to make life easier for both you and your dog, and to prevent things from getting worse. But if you want to make lasting changes in your dog's reactivity issues, you'll need to spend some time working on a training plan to address the problem.

This isn't as hard as it sounds, so don't panic. You'll need a friend to help out (or a few friends, if possible) and lots of tasty treats. If your dog is reactive toward other dogs rather than people, enlist a calm, friendly "helper dog" as well.

Finding a professional who can work with you in person can be extremely helpful, since he/she can help you set up the training environment for success. However, if you have to go it alone, you can still make lots of progress as long as you're careful and committed.

To train against leash reactivity:

1 ▸ GIVE YOUR DOG PLENTY OF SPACE

Start at a distance from your helper (ideally someone your dog doesn't know well, and/or a strange dog). You need to be far enough away that your dog is able to notice the helper without immediately reacting.

For some dogs, this means you need *lots* of distance at first. You can work in a large indoor area, outside in an open field, or on a quiet street. Take as much space as your dog needs to feel comfortable—whether it's 20 feet or an entire football field.

2 ▸ WAIT FOR HIM TO NOTICE

Watch your dog carefully, so that you can see the moment when he first notices the helper. As soon as he looks at them, praise and reward with a treat. If he's not interested in the food or you're unable to get his attention, this means you're too close. Move farther away from your helper and try again.

3 ▸ REWARD YOUR DOG

Continue to reward your dog every time he looks at the helper. Ideally, once he understands the game, this should move very quickly. He should eat his treat and immediately look back at your helper to earn another bite of food. When he's glancing quickly at the helper and then back at you for his treat with no barking at all, you're ready to move on to the next step.

4 ▸ TRY MOVING A BIT CLOSER

Small changes in distance can make a big difference, so watch your dog closely. Repeat step 3 several times. If your dog is still comfortable and relaxed, with no barking or intent staring at your helper, you can gradually continue moving nearer.

5 ▸ CLOSE THE GAP

Eventually, you should be able to stand just a few feet away from your helper while your dog stays relaxed and happy, taking treats from you without any trouble at all. Give yourself (and your pup) a pat on the back at this point—you're doing great!

The amount of time it takes to reach this step will vary from one dog to another. It might take a few weeks or a few months, or sometimes even longer; every dog is different. Go as slowly as needed. Rushing your dog will only set back your progress, so resist the temptation to try and hurry things along.

6 ▸ TRY IT AGAIN WITH SOMEONE NEW

Repeat steps 1–5 with a new helper, if possible. You may need to do this with several different people (and/or dogs) for your dog to get really comfortable with the process.

It can also be helpful to work in new locations. You can also ask your helper to change things up a bit if your dog is doing well—have him/her walk past you instead of standing still, or your helper can even smile and speak briefly to your dog as you approach.

7 ▸ ADD MORE CHALLENGES

Eventually, you want to simulate just about everything that you might encounter on a normal walk, so be creative. Just remember to take things slowly, and don't overwhelm your dog. If he seems nervous or gets too excited, just back up and make things easier for a bit, then try again.

SEPARATION ANXIETY

Let's face it: we all want our dogs to love us. Having a close bond with our canine companions is one of the greatest parts of dog ownership, for both humans and dogs. But what if your dog is so attached to you that he panics whenever he can't be with you?

Unfortunately, this is a reality that many pet parents deal with every day. If your dog barks or howls constantly while you're gone, destroys your walls or furniture, or has potty accidents that only happen when he's home alone, he may have separation anxiety.

As the name implies, this is a behavioral disorder that causes your dog to become incredibly stressed and upset whenever he's left alone. Separation anxiety can be a challenging problem to deal with, especially in severe cases. Some dogs cause thousands of dollars' worth of damage to their owners' homes, make so much noise that neighbors complain, or even injure themselves trying to escape a crate or room in which they're confined.

Fortunately, once the problem is recognized, there are lots of things you can do to help your pup feel more comfortable being home alone. With patience and consistency, most dog owners can make significant improvements in their pet's anxiety level, which makes life easier for everyone.

Coping with Separation Anxiety

To help your dog learn to cope with being home alone:

1 ▶ GET HIM NICE AND TIRED

Give your dog more exercise, especially just before you leave the house each day. While this won't solve an anxiety problem on its own, dogs who aren't getting sufficient exercise will often have more pent-up, nervous energy. This can contribute to panting, pacing, and crying when you leave.

To do a better job of this, adjust your schedule a bit if needed. Take your dog for a long walk in the morning before work or play a quick game of fetch in the backyard. If he's pleasantly tired from running and playing, he'll be much more likely to lay down for a nap once you're gone.

2 ▶ GIVE YOUR DOG MORE SPACE

Try allowing your pup to have more room to move around, if you're able to do this safely. For many dogs with separation anxiety, being confined in a crate or small room can increase their panic and make the problem worse.

Try leaving your dog loose in a larger part of the house while you're gone. In some cases, this can make a big difference in your dog's comfort level and dramatically improve his behavior.

3 ▸ SKIP THE DRAMA

Keep your arrivals and departures quiet and low-key. I know, this is tough for most of us. But giving long, dramatic goodbyes when you leave and celebrating with lots of excitement when you come home can make things worse. It only reinforces the idea that all the fun happens when you're there, and makes the house seem extra quiet and lonely after you leave.

Instead, be calm and matter-of-fact about entering and leaving the house. You can casually greet your dog when you get home, but go about your normal routine without paying much attention to him until he settles down.

4 ▸ LEAVE HIM WITH SOMETHING SPECIAL

Give your dog an extra-tasty, long-lasting treat each time you leave. Try puzzle toys such as a Twist 'n Treat stuffed with spray cheese, or a Kong packed full of kibble and peanut butter. Bully sticks or pig ears can also be good options for some dogs. This gives your pup something positive to look forward to and helps keep him busy while he's home alone.

5 ▸ MONITOR FROM AFAR

Use video recording technology to monitor your dog while you're gone. Video recording your dog while you're gone can be incredibly helpful, since this allows you to see changes in his anxiety level from day to day. You can then adjust your plan as needed, depending on what you see. Try using in-home surveillance equipment if you have some already, or use your tablet or webcam. You can also use a video camcorder on a tripod.

6 ▸ CONSIDER MEDICATION

Talk to your veterinarian about your pup's anxiety issues. This is especially important if your dog is causing significant damage to your home or injuring himself. For severe cases of separation anxiety, it can be very difficult to make progress at first without some prescription medication on board. Your vet can help you decide if this would be a good option for your pup and will prescribe an appropriate drug to help control his anxiety if needed.

THUNDERSTORM PHOBIA

There's no getting around it—thunderstorms can be scary, especially for dogs! Unpredictable claps of thunder and flashes of lightning are particularly unsettling for pups with a tendency toward anxiety or fear of loud noises, but over time any dog can develop a fear of storms.

Signs of thunderstorm phobia can range from mild behavioral changes like panting and pacing to more severe issues such as destroying walls or furniture in a panicked attempt to get away from the storm. This level of anxiety can be hard for many owners to live with, and is also very distressing for the dog, so it's well worth trying to help your pup with his fears, if you can.

Fortunately, there are several things you can do to help your dog learn that the world isn't ending when a thunderstorm rolls through. By providing some positive distractions and managing the environment to minimize his exposure to the scary sounds outside, you can make storms much more manageable for both of you.

Control Thunderstorm Phobia

To reduce your dog's anxiety during a thunderstorm:

1 ▶ PROVIDE SOME AMBIENT NOISE

Turn on the TV or radio before the storm starts to help mask the sounds of thunder. A white noise machine can also be used for this purpose.

2 ▶ BLOCK YOUR PUP'S VIEW

Close blinds or drapes in the house. For many dogs, seeing flashes of lightning outside makes their anxiety worse, because the lightning predicts scary booms of thunder shortly after.

3 ▶ GIVE HIM SOMEWHERE SAFE TO HIDE

Provide a safe haven for your dog to hide in during storms, if he wants to. There is no benefit to forcing him to stay out and "face his fears," so let him do whatever makes him comfortable.

Many dogs will choose a place themselves where they feel safe, such as in the bathtub or under the bed. If your pup does this on his own, it's fine to let him use the spot he already likes.

If your dog doesn't already have a preferred hiding place, try providing him with a crate covered in blankets so that it's dark inside and sounds are muffled. You could also try sitting with him in an interior room without any windows, such as a bathroom.

4 ▸ OFFER SOMETHING TASTY TO EAT

Try giving your dog a special treat or chew item as soon as the storm begins. A bully stick, pig ear, or a puzzle toy such as a Twist 'n Treat stuffed with canned food or spray cheese are all good options—experiment to see what your dog likes best. This will help to keep his mind off the thunder and over time can even teach him to associate good things with storms.

5 ▸ CONSIDER MEDICATION

If your pup's thunderstorm phobia is severe and he's having trouble coping even though you're doing everything you can, he might benefit from taking a prescription medication during storms. Your veterinarian can talk with you about short-acting antianxiety meds like alprazolam or trazodone to reduce your dog's fear and make it easier for him to cope.

DOG TRAINING TIP

Despite what you may have heard, there is no harm in comforting your pet if he's afraid. You are not "rewarding" anxiety by doing this, and you won't make the problem worse. Feel free to pet him, hold him on your lap, or let him snuggle with you during the storm if these things make him feel more secure. You can even try playing with your pup or doing some simple training exercises for treats while it's thundering outside, if he seems to enjoy this.

FEAR OR AGGRESSION AT VET VISITS

It's no secret that most dogs don't enjoy going to see the veterinarian. As many of us can probably relate, seeing the doctor isn't fun. But it's worse for pets, since they don't understand what's happening and why. Consider the visit from your dog's perspective:

The vet's office is full of strange smells and noises, unfamiliar dogs, and new people. This all adds up to a very challenging environment for a shy or anxious dog. It's also a place where scary things like shots and blood draws happen. If your pup has ever had surgery or been hospitalized for an injury or illness, he likely remembers these experiences also. This can make him stressed and worried as soon as he enters the clinic.

Fortunately, it doesn't have to be this way. There are several easy things you can do to help take the fear out of vet visits. With practice, many dogs can even learn to enjoy seeing the vet and cooperate happily with their exam, rather than cowering under the chairs or growling at the doctor. This makes life easier for everyone: your pup, the veterinary staff, and you!

Reduce Fear or Aggression at Vet Visits

To help your dog learn to enjoy visiting the vet's office:

1 ▸ BRING SNACKS

Take along a supply of tasty treats for your pup to eat during the visit. Honestly, for most dogs, this is the simplest thing you can do to help the appointment go smoothly, but it's something that most owners don't think about.

Pack a baggie of whatever your pup likes best. Cheese, hot dog slices, or small soft commercial dog treats are all good options. Ask every staff member at the clinic to feed your dog a few treats when they say hello. You can also keep your dog busy with a handful of tasty snacks in front of his nose while he gets his exam and vaccines.

2 ▸ TEACH YOUR DOG TO STAND STILL

This skill makes the veterinary visit much easier, since your dog will know how stand and stay calm while being touched and handled all over. Make sure to reward him generously when he stands calmly for the doctor. See Six Steps to Standing Still for a Physical Exam in Part III for more information on how to teach this skill.

3 ▸ MUZZLE TRAIN YOUR DOG

Teach your pup to be comfortable wearing a muzzle, especially if he has a history of being fearful or aggressive with veterinary staff. There may be times at the vet's office when he needs to wear a muzzle for safety. If he's never been introduced to one before, this can be very stressful and scary. See Eight Steps to Muzzle Training in Part III for detailed instructions on muzzle training.

4 ▸ STOP IN FOR "HAPPY VISITS"

Happy visits are quick trips to the vet's office where nothing bad happens and your dog gets lots of treats and petting. This is a great way to help him associate good things with the veterinary clinic. You want him to come prancing happily up to the door, rather than slinking along the ground or having to be carried in.

5 ▸ PLAN AHEAD TO AVOID PROBLEMS

Talk with your vet about any specific concerns you might have, and make a plan to help the visit go smoothly. This is especially important if your dog has a history of being aggressive or difficult to handle at the vet's office.

For example, you may be able to arrange to bring in your pup first thing in the morning when the lobby is empty, and go straight back to the treatment area for vaccines or other procedures. This allows your dog to get in and out quickly, without the added stress of sitting in a group of strange dogs and people in the waiting room.

Pre-medicating at home with antianxiety meds (or even injectable sedation in the office) can also be a good way of reducing stress in some cases. Your veterinarian should be happy to discuss options for making your dog more comfortable—so just ask.

CAR-RIDE ANXIETY

If your dog gets nervous or upset about riding in the car, you're not alone. Car-ride anxiety is a common problem that can make life difficult for many pet owners. It's hard to take your pup to the park, a training class, or even his yearly vet visit if he seems to have a panic attack every time you load him up for a ride.

The good news is, if you're willing to put in a little time and effort, this is usually a fairly straightforward issue to solve. Most dogs can eventually learn to tolerate or even enjoy car rides without any fear or anxiety, which makes things much easier for both of you.

Get Over Car-Ride Anxiety

To train your dog to ride calmly in the car:

1 ▸ SET THE STAGE

Start with your dog on-leash and have a good supply of very high-value treats. Pieces of cheese, chicken, roast beef, or hot dog slices work best for this exercise.

2 ▸ WALK YOUR DOG OVER TO THE CAR

Stand beside the car door where you usually load him up, and feed several treats in a row. Don't open the door or attempt to put him in the car yet. It's important to go slowly and make sure he's comfortable at every step before moving on.

3 ▸ REPEAT STEP 2 SEVERAL TIMES

Take a break before going any further. If your dog is very nervous, you may need to spend a few separate training sessions on this step before progressing any further. If so, that's okay. Take as much time as you need for your pup to be happy and relaxed when you approach the car together.

4 ▸ TRY GETTING IN THE CAR

Once your dog is comfortable, open the car door and encourage him to hop in. If he does, immediately praise and reward. If not, place a treat within easy reach on the seat and allow him to reach up and eat it. Do this several times, until he's comfortable enough to jump in.

At this stage, your dog may jump back out of the car as soon as he eats the treat. This is fine! Don't attempt to close the door or force him to stay inside. As he gets more comfortable with this exercise, he will be more willing to relax and stay in the car for longer periods.

If your dog is very small or has physical limitations that prevent him from jumping, you can gently lift him into the car instead. Give several treats in a row with lots of praise, then immediately let him out again.

5 ▸ CLOSE THE DOOR

When your dog is happy eating treats in the car for up to ten seconds at a time, try closing the door behind him after he jumps in. Praise and reward generously, then let him out again.

6 ▸ TURN ON THE ENGINE

Ask your dog to hop into the car, shut the door behind him, get in the driver's seat, and start the car. Praise and give him several treats, then turn the car off and let him out. Do this a few times, until you're sure that your dog is calm and happy with the engine running.

7 ▸ START DRIVING

At this point, you can begin to move the car a short distance. Try backing out of the driveway first—then return, stop the car, and let your dog out.

Once you reach this stage, it's best to have a helper who can sit in the back seat and reward your dog with treats while the car moves. This leaves you free to concentrate on driving. If you don't have a helper available, try giving your dog a Kong toy stuffed with spray cheese or canned dog food to eat while you drive.

8 ▸ GO A LITTLE FARTHER

Gradually work up to driving around the block, then try short trips to nearby places like a park, pet store, or fast food drive-thru where your pup can get a special treat. All of this helps him learn to associate good things with car rides.

9 ▸ WORK UP TO REAL-LIFE TRIPS

Eventually, you should be able to go on longer trips to other places, like the vet's office or groomer. Just make sure to reward your pup every now and then for riding calmly, even after this skill is learned.

SHYNESS WITH NEW PEOPLE

Just like us, dogs have different personalities: some are friendly social butterflies who love everyone, while others are anxious or worried around strangers. If your pup gets nervous about meeting new people, don't worry. There are some easy things you can do to help.

Overcoming Shyness with New People

To teach your dog to be more comfortable with new people:

1 ▸ LISTEN TO YOUR DOG

This is important! Never force an anxious dog to hold still and allow petting, and never pressure him to approach and "say hi" to a stranger if he doesn't want to. Not only will this make his anxiety worse over time, it can lead to aggression if your pup feels compelled to defend himself. If he wants to be left alone, respect his choice.

2 ▸ REWARD FOR LOOKING AT PEOPLE

If your dog shows interest in meeting someone, encourage this by praising and rewarding him each time he looks at the person. Allow him to move closer if he wants to approach. Just make sure that the choice is his.

If he'd rather watch from a distance instead of directly interacting with strangers, this is okay too. Just praise and offer a treat each time he looks. This will help him associate seeing new people with good things, even if he isn't ready for an actual greeting just yet.

3 ▸ HAVE A NEW FRIEND TOSS SOME TREATS

If the person is willing to help, offer her or him a handful of tasty treats. Ask the person to toss the treats on the ground, one at a time, for your dog to eat. This is another way of helping your pup learn that interacting with strangers can be fun.

It's always best for the other person to toss the treats, rather than attempting to feed your dog from the hand. This is because hand-feeding can put a lot of pressure on the dog to come closer than he wants to in order to get the food. This can often backfire and create more anxiety. Instead, tossing the treats from a distance allows your pup to eat them easily and enjoy the interaction with no strings attached.

4 ▸ READ YOUR DOG

Watch your dog's body language to see what he wants to do next. If he doesn't want to approach the person, say thanks and move on. He will get more confident over time, as he learns to associate people with good things.

5 ▸ KEEP GREETINGS CALM AND NONTHREATENING

If your pup seems relaxed and wants to say hello, you can let him approach. The other person can help the greeting go more smoothly by avoiding direct eye contact, crouching down rather than leaning over your pup, and petting him on the chest or under the chin. If your dog greets successfully, praise him and give a reward. This is a big step for many shy dogs.

6 ▸ BUILD HIS CONFIDENCE

Over time, with practice, your pup should become less anxious and more relaxed around new people. You will also become more proficient at reading his body language to make sure he's comfortable, which is just as important. He may never be an outgoing, friendly dog who loves to say hi—and that's okay. But by giving gentle encouragement and respecting his choices, you can help him learn to get along more easily in a world full of strangers.

COMPULSIVE BEHAVIORS

For some dog owners, it might come as a surprise to learn that dogs can suffer from a problem that is similar to obsessive-compulsive disorder (OCD) in humans. Typical signs of this issue include repetitive behavior patterns such as spinning, chasing their tails, "fly-biting" (snapping at the air), flank sucking, excessively licking objects, light or shadow chasing, or even self-mutilation.

For most dogs, these behaviors begin as a coping response brought on by stress, frustration, or anxiety, similar to the way that humans might twist their hair or bite their nails. If your pup only does these things when he's overly excited or nervous, it's likely nothing to worry about. However, if he's doing them constantly, even when nothing much is happening, this is more concerning.

Fortunately, with time and patience, it's often possible to help dogs with compulsive behavioral issues. So if your pup is doing these things, don't despair. Just take steps to start working on the problem, and consider finding a professional to help you in person if needed.

Managing Compulsive Behaviors

To reduce your dog's tendency to "get stuck" in compulsive behavior patterns:

1 ▸ GET A CHECKUP FROM YOUR VET

Many of the behaviors noted here can be caused by nerve pain, allergies, skin problems, or neurologic abnormalities. If your pup has a physical issue causing the abnormal behavior, this will need to be diagnosed and treated in order to get the problem under control.

2 ▸ GET YOUR PUP MORE EXERCISE

Increase the amount of exercise your dog gets each day. Add an extra walk or high-energy play session, or sign up for a reward-based obedience or agility class to help tire him out. While this won't solve the problem on its own, a tired dog has far less nervous energy to expend and is much more likely to settle down for a nap during "downtime" at home.

3 ▸ KEEP HIS BRAIN BUSY

Give your dog a puzzle toy or something to chew on, especially if he seems bored or restless. This helps by giving him some extra mental stimulation and providing him with a fun activity to keep him occupied, which leaves less time for compulsive spinning, licking, etc.

4 ▶ TEACH AN ALTERNATE BEHAVIOR

Identify situations that tend to trigger the compulsive behavior and teach your dog to do something different when they happen. For example, if he gets upset and starts spinning in circles every morning when the mailman comes, teach him to grab a toy instead or to go to his bed for a treat.

5 ▶ REDIRECT TO SOMETHING ELSE

If you see your dog starting to engage in one of his compulsions, interrupt him and redirect to some other activity. For a dog who chases lights and shadows, for example, you could call him to you for a treat as soon as you see him start to fixate on something, then take him out for a walk, start a game of fetch, or give him a chew toy instead.

If you're unable to get your dog's attention once he gets stuck in his behavior pattern, consider having him wear a head halter and lightweight drag line in the house. This allows you to physically interrupt him by gently controlling his head, so that you can more easily redirect him to something else.

6 ▶ CONSIDER MEDICATION

For dogs with severe compulsive behavioral issues, prescription medication may be a necessary part of their treatment plan. If you're having trouble making progress with training alone, talk with your veterinarian about meds that might be helpful in getting things under control.

SHOULD YOU CONSIDER MEDICATION?

The topic of behavioral medication for dogs can be controversial, but it's an incredibly important topic, so I want to address it briefly here. As a veterinarian who often works with behavioral cases, I can attest to the fact that pharmacologic intervention definitely has its place.

Will starting your dog on meds fix his behavioral problem, without any further work on your part?

No, of course not.

But for some dogs, particularly those with serious behavioral issues like aggression or anxiety, the use of an appropriate medication as part of their overall treatment plan can be tremendously helpful.

Commonly used medications in the field of veterinary behavior include the following:

- Selective serotonin reuptake inhibitors (SSRIs), such as Prozac, Paxil, and Zoloft
- Tricyclic antidepressants (TCAs), such as Clomicalm and Elavil
- Short-acting antianxiety drugs, such as Xanax and trazodone
- Sedatives, such as Sileo and acepromazine

Depending on your dog's specific problem, your veterinarian may recommend one of these medications (or a combination of meds, in some cases) as an adjunct treatment option along with a well thought-out training plan. If you have concerns about risks or side effects, or are unsure of how your vet expects the medication to help, don't be afraid to ask.

Of course, not every dog with a behavioral problem will require prescription meds. If your pup's issues are fairly minor, or if you're seeing significant improvement with training alone, drugs may not offer any additional benefits.

FOUR STEPS TO

Determine If You Should Consider Medication

So how can you know if using medication is a choice you should think about for your dog? Generally speaking, medication should be considered as a possible treatment option in the following situations:

1 ▸ **PATHOLOGICAL BEHAVIORAL PROBLEMS VERSUS TRAINING ISSUES**

This is an important distinction to make. Meds can be a helpful option for dogs with behavioral issues that are genuinely abnormal: serious aggression, anxiety, reactivity, and so forth. They are not appropriate for simple training problems, such as jumping or leash pulling, or for behaviorally normal dogs with "too much" energy.

2 ▸ **SEVERE SITUATIONAL ANXIETY**

This is the type of fearful behavior commonly seen in dogs with separation anxiety or thunderstorm phobia. These dogs have something akin to a panic response when storms roll in or when their owner leaves for work. Their blood stream is flooded with stress hormones, their heart rate increases, they pant and salivate uncontrollably, and so on. If these biological changes aren't controlled, then it's very difficult to make any significant progress with training. Medication can be a very useful aid for this.

3 ▸ ISSUES THAT IMPACT QUALITY OF LIFE

If your pup is so anxious that he has trouble relaxing, even at home when things are quiet, medication might make a big difference in how comfortable he is. The same is true for reactivity problems that affect what activities he can participate in. It's also true for car-ride anxiety, because this condition places limits on where he's able to go.

4 ▸ DIFFICULTY MAKING PROGRESS

Even if your pup's behavioral problem doesn't seem all that severe, a lack of improvement with consistent training is often a red flag that things are more serious than you thought. If you've been working on your dog's issues for weeks or months without making much headway, consider talking to your vet. Meds may improve his ability to focus and learn, which means the rest of your treatment plan will be much more effective.

NATURAL MEDICATION ALTERNATIVES

In addition to the medications previously noted, there are a number of natural products and over-the-counter supplements that can be helpful for some dogs—these can be used on their own or in combination with prescription meds.

Keep in mind that in most cases, the effects of these products will be fairly subtle, so don't expect miracles, especially if you're not doing anything else to address the problem. But as an adjunct treatment option along with a solid training plan (and possibly medication from your vet, if needed), they can definitely help.

FOUR STEPS TO

Consider for Using Alternative Medication

Some natural products can have a useful role in treating behavioral issues. They include:

1 ▸ DOG APPEASING PHEROMONE (DAP)

DAP is a synthetic version of the pheromone that mother dogs make when they nurse their puppies. For most dogs, it's associated with memories of comfort and relaxation. Studies have shown effectiveness in reducing anxiety for dogs with thunderstorm phobia, separation anxiety, and a number of other behavioral issues.

In the United States, DAP is marketed under the trade names Adaptil and Comfort Zone. It can be used in the form of a plug-in wall diffuser, a collar, or a spray. Follow label instructions for each type of product to ensure best results.

2 ▸ ESSENTIAL OILS

Just as in humans, certain types of essential oils such as lavender, peppermint, and orange can have a calming effect on anxious or overly excited dogs. Make sure to consult your veterinarian for instructions on safe usage if you opt to give this a try, as essential oils can be irritating or even toxic in high concentrations, or if they are used improperly.

3 ▶ THUNDERSHIRT OR ANXIETY WRAP

These products are wraps or doggy "T-shirts" that are designed to fit snugly when the pet is wearing them. The resulting effect of feeling pressure all over the body is relaxing for some dogs, similar to swaddling for newborn babies or weighted blankets for grown humans. They can be used on an as-needed basis for thunderstorm or noise phobias, scary events such as veterinary visits, or even as part of everyday life for dogs with generalized anxiety issues.

4 ▶ CALMING SUPPLEMENTS

In recent years, a number of effective antianxiety supplements have been developed for use in dogs. These products can be purchased over the counter without a prescription and are generally composed of safe, natural calming ingredients such as L-theanine, L-tryptophan, casein, C3 (Colostrum Calming Complex), and flower extracts.

Be aware that the US Food and Drug Administration (FDA) does not monitor nutritional supplements for quality or effectiveness, so I recommend sticking with well-studied, brand-name products from reputable veterinary manufacturers. Some good options to consider include Composure Pro (VetriScience), Solliquin (Nutramax Laboratories), and Zylkene (Vetoquinol).

INDEX

ABOUT THE AUTHOR

Jennifer Summerfield is a veterinarian and professional dog trainer based in Huntington, West Virginia. She teaches group classes and private lessons in basic obedience for pet dogs, and also coaches students getting started in dog sports such as agility and obedience. In her veterinary practice, she works with dogs with a variety of serious behavioral issues including aggression to humans or other animals, separation anxiety, and compulsive behavioral disorders.

Outside of work, Dr. Summerfield enjoys competing in AKC agility, rally, conformation, and competitive obedience with her three Shetland sheepdogs. She has been a past webinar presenter for the professionally acclaimed Academy for Dog Trainers and a guest lecturer on clinical animal behavior for veterinary technician students at her local community college, and also writes a blog on behavior and training issues for dog owners.